This
book
Belongs
to _____
- - - - - - - - - -

RUBBISH
IT'S WHAT
EVERYBODY'S
TALKING

43 RAINHAM ROAD
KENSAL GREEN
NW1 DL
LONDON

Contents

February 16th 2006

1

RUBBISH

RUBBISH
IT'S WHAT
EVERYBODY'S
TALKING

43 RAINHAM ROAD
KENSAL GREEN
NW10 5DL
LONDON

London, _____ February 16th _____ 200 __6__

EDITOR IN CHIEF Jenny Dyson

DEPUTY EDITOR Jack Dyson

ART DIRECTION AND DESIGN HarrimanSteel www.harrimansteel.co.uk

ASSOCIATE EDITOR Cat Callender

FASHION DIRECTOR John Alfredo Harris

FASHION EDITORS Claire Durbridge, Mary Fellowes, Alba Hodsoll, Romilly Mason, Flynn Roddam

PHOTOGRAPHERS Julian Broad, Thomas Brodin, Chris Brooks, Tara Darby, Zac Frackelton, Lee Jenkins, Craig Lynn, Jason Pietra, Ithaka Roddam

ILLUSTRATORS Sarah Doyle, Jessie Ford, Alice Tait, George Wu

RUBBISH CORRESPONDENTS Toby Andersen, Simon Chilvers, Florence Dixon, Marc Hare, Mary Killen, Priscilla Kwateng, Dan Lywood, Myfanwy Moore, Naomi Nevitt, Diane Pernet, Alistair Scott, Valentine Warner, Antonia Whyatt

FRONT COVER
Erin O'Connor is photographed by Julian Broad. Necklace created by Solange Azagury-Partridge. Sardine tin hairclip created by Jonathan Anderson. Corset by Aquascutum, (with thanks to Claire Durbridge). Fashion editor Jenny Dyson, Makeup by Karen Alder using Becca, Hair by Paul Percival @ Phamous. Still life of frame and wallpaper photographed by Zac Frackelton. Wallpaper designed by Jessie Ford

ISBN: 0-9552172-0-2

Published by RUBBISH Ltd, Unregistered trademark c 2005
RUBBISH Magazine, 43 Rainham Road, London NW10 5DL www.RUBBISHmag.com
For all RUBBISH Enquiries +44 (0) 7811 396 332 or email info@RUBBISHmag.com

Distributed by Art Data www.artdata.co.uk +44 (0)20 87471061 and Printed by Mondadori Printing

(ed's note: this magazine is printed on half-recycled paper. Whole recycled is really expensive. Being green costs money, you know!)

RUBBISH
IT'S
EV
LKING

43 RAINHAM ROAD
KENSAL GREEN
NW10 5DL
LONDON

RUBBISH

RUBBISH Editor's Letter

London, February 16 2006

3

Dear reader,

Welcome to issue one of RUBBISH, the brand new fashion annual dedicated to the silly side of style, packed with all manner of bonkers stories, scribbles and satire.

There is a seriousness to fashion that jars with life as we at RUBBISH HQ know it. Is it possible to be chic and funny? Can you be simultaneously cool and amusing? Do you have to be serious to be stylish? Exactly why is it that everybody takes fashion so darn seriously? These are some of the extremely insignificant things we have explored while compiling our debut issue. RUBBISH is your refreshing antidote to the heady, gloss, glamour and shine so vital to being conventionally hip. Badly dressed? who cares! We're here to tip fashion on its head, have a side-splitting laugh and celebrate the consequences.

When it comes to fashion mags, the written word is often a mere afterthought to the image; a PS to the way in which stories are put together when you might as well just have blah blah rhubarb rhubarb custard written beside a fashion image (although that actually sounds rather good, no?). Inside RUBBISH, words and pictures get equal billing and that's something we want to celebrate.

We would love to hear from you and look forward to receiving mountains of letters, emails, pictures, doodles and ideas. Hopefully they'll be so bad we'll just have to include them in our upcoming features to-do list for issue two, due out later this year. We are also launching a website to serve as a fashionable forum in between issues. Log on, check it out and get contributing. And please, spread the word. RUBBISH, it's what everybody's talking!

xJenny

RUBBISH

RUBBISH
IT'S WHAT
EVERYBODY'S
TALKING

43 RAINHAM ROAD
KENSAL GREEN
NW10 5DL
LONDON

London, February 16 2006

Contri

4

Thandie Newton
Actress + Fashionable
Person

Simon
Attfield
Comedian

Flynn Roddam
Teen Stylist

Toby Andersen
Resident Poet

Ithaka
Roddam
Teen Photographer

Romilly Mason
Stylist

Julian Dickenson
Creative Director

Alice Tait
Illustrator

Nova Dando
Knitter

Claire Durbridge
Stylist

Caroline
Cabbold
toaster magician

Tara Darby
Photographer

Antonia
Whyatt
Beauty Writer

Chris
Brookes
Photographer

Nick Steel
Creative Director

Jessie Ford Illustrator

RUBBISH

RUBBISH
IT'S WHAT
EVERYBODY'S
TALKING

43 RAINHAM ROAD
KENSAL GREEN
NW10 5DL
LONDON

Mutiny

London, February 16th 200 6

5

Rebecca Miller
Photographer

John Alfredo Harris
Fashion Editor

Julian Vogel
Rubbish PR

Alisa Hodsoll
Teen Stylist

Florence Dixon
Teen Writer

Solange Azagury-Partridge
Rubbish Jewellery designer

Danny Sangra
Designer

Max Hare
Music Correspondant

Mary Fellowes
Stylist

Aaye Blegvad
Vegetable Stylist

Thomas Brodin
Photographer

Matt Bleare
Designer

George W.
Art Director

Dan Burn-Forti
Photographer

Jack Dyson
Deputy Editor

Jenny Dyson
Editor

Valentine Warner
Catering Correspondant

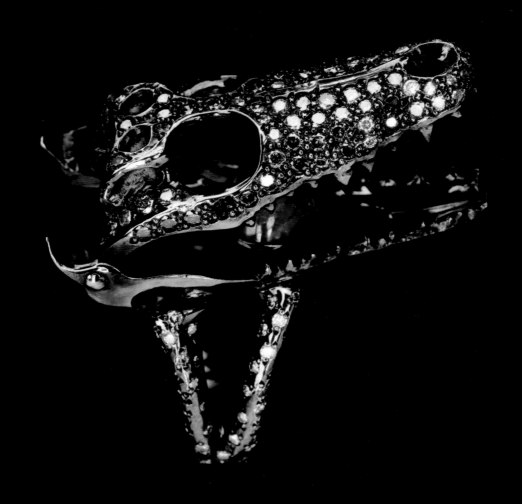

CROC SKULL RING

SOLANGE AZAGURY-PARTRIDGE

WWW.SOLANGE.INFO   TEL.NO: +44 (0) 207 792 0197   EMAIL: INFO@SOLANGE.INFO

BLUE BIRD RING

SOLANGE AZAGURY-PARTRIDGE

WWW.SOLANGE.INFO TEL.NO: +44 (0) 207 792 0197 EMAIL: INFO@SOLANGE.INFO

8

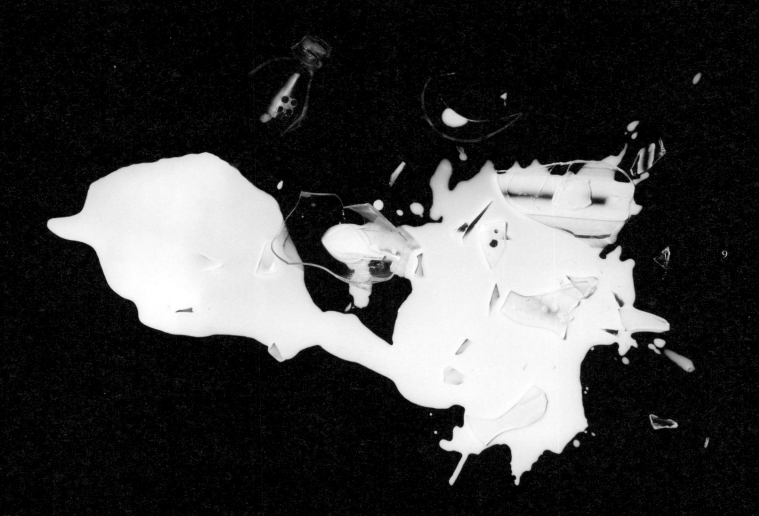

Domestic Knits

Photography by Jason Pietra
Couture domestic objects knitted and created by Nova Dando

1. Mop

10

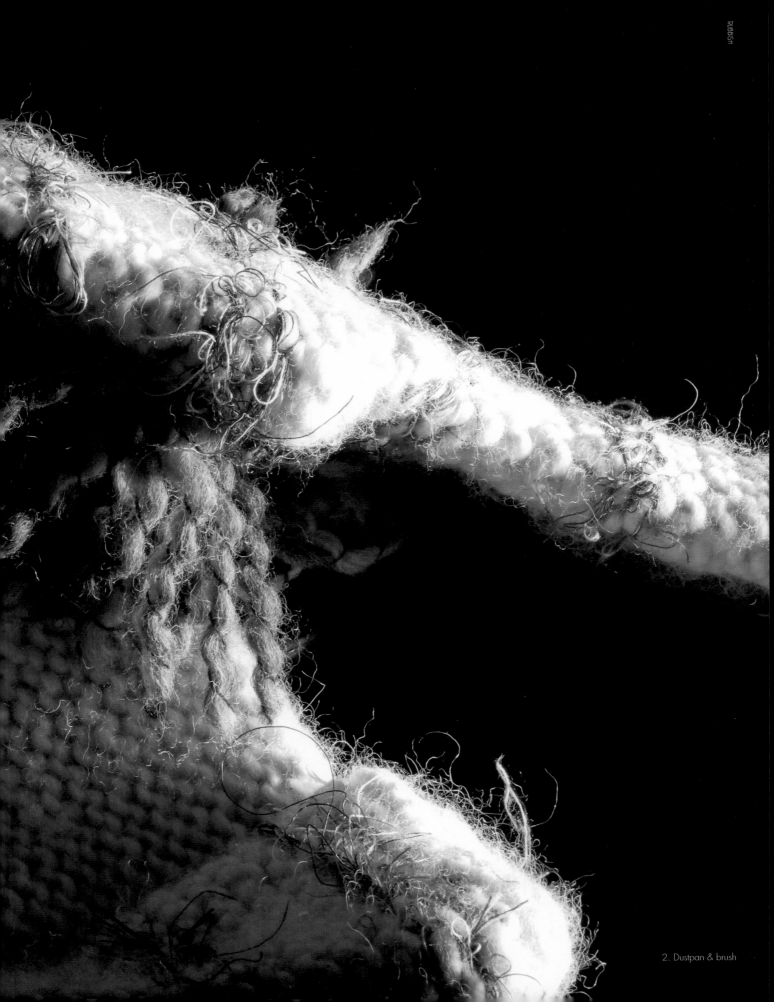

2. Dustpan & brush

Being Matthew

Arm candy to the most beautiful women in the world, fashion designer to the jet set and the gorgeous, Matthew Williamson is just the kind of guy we all aspire to be, or at least have in our repertoire of mates. Simon Chilvers and Priscilla Kwateng carried out a fashiontific experiment to see just what it really takes to live the life of Matthew Williamson and muse to experience his wonderful, chic world just for one day. Photography by *Chris Brooks*.

Mr Williamson has always courted stars to showcase his work and, unsurprisingly, it's working jolly well for him. His relationship with lady celebrities is a marriage of mutual convenience: He attracts an entourage of lovely ladies, clung tightly to him for swinging fashion dos, dressed by him, resulting in that all important photo-mo. And it is this very photo-mo which boosts his business more than any glossy ad in Vogue could ever hope to. His irresistible good looks and personal sense of style makes him hot date material plus - and it's a big plus - the gay factor helps, as the ladies' boyfriends can have a night off, safe in the knowledge that their partner's date is not going to try and snog them at the end of the evening.

Not surprisingly, this kind of hob knobbing has resulted in the man himself becoming a celeb in his own goddamn right. Far be it for us to speculate but we think that without his courtship and guidance, certain starlets would be up shit style creek without a paddle. Naturally the designer and muse relationship is beneficial to both parties but surely this demonstrates that it is Matthew who is the true icon, non?

But just how do you work it, Matthew style?

Priscilla Kwateng, left
and Simon Chilvers, right,
ponder the ways of Williamson.

13

. Getting Matthew's Look

Mr Williamson's attire looks effortlessly thrown together. But it isn't. Firstly, his signature shade of purple ain't easily found on the British high-stree
Gap's super-smashing-great purple polo had sold out in XS by the beginning of winter (apparently everyone is buying them a size smaller so the
it is snug – how very Matthew?) and not even the jolly helpful Gap press office could come to the rescue. Secondly, the combination of the ver
ou courant flouncy scarf (or pashmina), velvet blazer, brogues and lashings of (fake) tan may look great on him but it all added up to make Rubbish Matthew
eel like an overdressed nonce. Don't even get Rubbish Matthew started on that freaking facial hair. Hours of (not) fun scraping in the bathroom, and fo
what? To get a strip of growth to grace yours truly's face that looked vaguely (emphasis on vaguely) like his. With the bold colour trend for men this yea
nd purple looking so big for boys for last season the influence of Matthew is everywhere in menswear. Question: where's the men's line, Matt?

13.00 hours, the Wolseley for lunch

16.00 hours, a quick peek at the store

16.00 hours, a VIM (very important meeting) outside Vogue House

18.00 hours, back to the studio

15

2. Find a Boho-like Muse

Think Matthew, think Kelis. Think major fro. Think frizzy wig ain't going over these braids. Think again. Fortunately our friendly high street took a leaf (or is that a whole tree?) out of Matthew's boho bible for spring/summer 2005 and had sewing machines whizzing up tributes aplenty – hence the abundance of Sienna slaves trogged up in one element or another, likely to include one of the following: printed sundresses replete with ruffled tiered skirt, crocheted cardies or retro waistcoats. Lucky them. Rubbish Matthew's muse went the whole frigging hog. Naturally huge sunglasses worn indoors are uber essential. Glum expression on the other hand... that's optional.

3. Have a Glam Lunch

Those poor folks at The Wolseley didn't quite know what had hit them. Expecting: Matthew and guest. Arriving: Two crazies in shades. Professionalism being their forte, however, not a flinch was to be had, just a friendly welcome before being escorted to our table, surrounded by curious onlookers and a suspicious maitre d. Surgically attached shades avec le crazy frock guaranteed most diners thought Rubbish Matthew, as he supped the champers and chuffed on the fag, had ordered a proper plate of loony for his lunching companion.

4. Make a Tour of your Store

How the jumped-up boutique shop assistants failed to recognise the very designer behind the togs they flog is really quite beyond us. As we flicked through racks of dresses at Matthew's flagship store on Bruton Street, the shop girls saw fit to snigger behind our backs. Resolutely, Rubbish Matthew spotted a bag out of place and moved it before holding up a snazzy little number against his new muse's bosom. Later, an 'anonymous' caller contacted the store posing as a reporter who'd been offered a paparazzi shot of 'Matthew' with a young, unidentified black lady. Could they perhaps shed some light as to who she was? Could they hell. "Sorry" they sniffed, "Matthew hasn't been in today."

5. From Percy Street Office to Vogue House to Home Home [of course meaning Primrose Hill darlings], for a quick shoot for a simply darling new magazine. Click, click, flash, flash. Oh, what's this we have here then? "Your camera's ill bruv," interrupts a passerby. "Are you models or what?" No darling – we are Matthew and Muse. Show us some respect. Click! Click! Click!

Next issue: Being John Galliano

New Suzy!

No Fashion nouse?
FEAR NOT!

Simply cut out this **FABULOUS** **SUZY MENKES** quiff

Colour in with black ink pen or crayon and attach to forehead with string.

Gives you instant style radar and takes you straight to **WHERE IT'S AT!**

FASHION FRINGE

Next issue: The Katie (Grand)

No. 1

Exclusives, views and
entirely made up news.

THE BUGLE

by Valentine Warner

CAKETASTROPHE

CHEF ~in~ CAKE baking SHOCKER!

Illustration by Alice Tait

18

ONTENTS

Chef in cake disaster

19

THE MOST RUBBISH CAKE I EVER MADE

**EXCLUSIVE
BY CATERING GOD
VALENTINE WARNER.**

H ad it not been for the fact that at the time I had one of Australia's best cakeologists working for me, I would never have let this happen. Vol au vents? Make them in my sleep. Entire evening's worth of canapes in red and black? Did that for YSL. Mini enchiladas for 300 at 24 hour's notice? I'm there with the chilis, doing my gringo best.

Anyway, there I was, poncing around in my velvet jacket at some Nothing Hill soiree when I bumped into a certain celebrated young stylist and mademoiselle of what is right and proper. After the politities, she asked if I might like to make a cake for a Royal grandchild's fifth birthday. It was her present as the godmother, to be delivered at Kensington palace in three days at 3pm precisely.

SCREAMING

"C an we have it in the shape of a rocket?" she asked. Champagne making me overexcited, I was straight in there. "Of course, anything you want. What about a rocket like the one Tintin went to the moon in? It can have a launch made of angelica and meringue smoke blasting out as if to lift off above the wide eyed littluns."

The details went on and the godmother's face lit up. The commission was secure. So confident was I in Deborah's talents as a gateau crafting genius that I would challenge anyone to spot the difference between a real stuffed otter and one she had manipulated out of chocolate, sponge and praline. I give Debs a copy of Destination Moon the following morning, point at the rocket and say 'make that'. "No problem, girlfriend," she says, stuffing the Tintin book in her bag of piping nozzles and icing magazines.

Later on that day, I put a call in to check how the cake is coming along. "Oh fine, just don't worry." Hasty call of my own a while later. "Debs, how's the cake? Only two days, you know." "Jeez, you worry too much girlfriend, I can do it with my eyes closed."

So now I'm not worried. Comes the day, and it transpires that Debs has gone walkabout the night before around various Australian watering holes and makes a flimsy attempt at hiding the fact she feels rough as a wombat's ass crusted in mud and twigs. She'll be at the kitchen in 20 minutes, so I strategically decide not to hassle her. She'll punch on through, she's never let me down, I say to myself over and over.

Noon. Another phone check. It seems everything is running with NASA like precision and I needn't have worried.

Fifty minutes later something pulls me towards a decision to pay a surprise visit to my queen of cakes. I bound into the kitchen full of praise for the sugary artwork even a child of royal lineage would be spoilt to receive. I walk in on what throws me into precipitous panic. We have one hour to deliver a splendid cake that really does look like the person who made it had their eyes closed. "Val, this has never happened to me before." Debs' jaw is gritted, her cheeks are flushed and my nostrils are flaring. Having made a new year's decision to try and be less psychotic and to keep drama at bay, I gently ask if we can sort it. She says it is rectifiable.

"Should I stay and help or will I make you nervous?" I leave her mixing new icing. After nipping home to smoke half a packet of cigarettes and blot out the panic with a few heavy techno tracks, 45 minutes later I return. It's all gone fucko. I act without sensitivity. Debs looks wounded and cross as I pull the cake, the icing, the pots, racks, spoons into the bin with a wild sweep of the arm. Insult to injury. "Relax Debs, clean up this war zone, have a fag and make some red icing. I'm going to Sainsbury's, back soon."

Back from the supermarket and life is really not tasting better, we crack on with plan B: To make a rocket cake plug two Swiss rolls end to end with a chopstick. Place one upside-down ice cream cone atop and ice the whole fucker in red. Then stick in three crude fins fashioned from cardboard cutouts wrapped in tin foil. Eh voila! Next, axe the launch stand altogether and gather broken meringue around base of rocket hoping it will be observed as smoke.

"OK Debs, let's go. We are out of time and this is the cake they are gonna get. We'll stop and buy some white ribbon and wind it round the rocket to make it stripy."

20

CURSING

RANTING

We stop for the ribbon and moments later turn into Millionaires' row with me in the back trying to keep the cake upright. Three speed bumps later, the cake now looks more like a skinned rhino's chap than a rocket, slowly lowering its head down into its box. Even the cake is embarrassed. Shit. "Don't worry, we'll get it rampant again with some steadying ribbon."

Ashamed of my creation on exiting the car I put my jacket over the box and approach security.

"Could you tell us what's in the box sir?" ask two constables.
"A rocket cake for the Royal's birthday."
"Sorry sir, but we'll have to verify that. Would you mind showing us?"
I pull back the jacket and they peer in, instantly bursting into giggles they can barely repress.
"A rocket is it, sir? Are you sure, sir?
Carry on, sir," giggle, smirk, nudge.

So we carry the cake towards fresh horrors. There at the front door is the whole family literally jumping up and down gleefully whooping 'the cake! the cake! It's arrived!'. My heart sinks more and I pull the jacket back over the box.

I ask to be taken to the cake's party location and insist on no peeking until we have made the finishing touches. I feel like an impostor as they look even more excited. We plug in the fin,(yes, the other two have got lost on the way), hastily break out the ribbon and start winding it around what now looks like nursery school mess. It perks up, slowly becoming a rocket. Just. Deborah then asks me to put my finger in the knot, to secure the ribbon. God knows how, but horror of horrors she pulls the knot garrotting the rocket cake clean in half. The top falls off and into a polar bear rug. Deep calm sweeps over me as lean down, pick up the thing and pluck the polar hair from the still sticky icing goo. I bend towards Deborah's ear and quietly whisper to her that we are leaving. Now. No goodbyes.

I wedge the top back on the bottom. Tie over the wound with ribbon, cluster the broken meringue and leave with royal voices approaching from nearby corridors, adrenalin urging me to break from a panicky but dignified walk into a run.

Safely back on high street Kensington I pull over and freak out. Screaming, ranting, cursing, blaspheming torrents of vile poison at Deborah. How could I, ever live this down? This is the worst day of my life in culinary terms and it's All Her fault. On seeing Debs' blank expressionless face, something odd happens. I start laughing. We both do and before long we are leaning head to head against each other, laughter hurting our stomachs and tears flooding my car interior. The next morning I send a hundred quid's worth of white tulips to my poor friend the godmother. She hasn't spoken to me since, but if anyone needs a cake… anyone?

Hello?

BLASPHEMING

21

California has just passed a law
to ban body hair in public spaces,
writes our Hollywood correspondent.
The glimpsing of A-list underarm
hair at a recent Vanity Hair party
triggered riots among beauticians and
spa workers of southern California,
resulting in more than ten tonnes
of warm wax being deliberately poured
down Sunset Boulevard during rush
hour. "There were hairy people
everywhere, being really hairy.
It was really scary," says one
eye witness.

body
hair
ban to
commence

Surprising opposers to this ban include
Michael Jackson's monkey Bubbles,
the actor Hugh Jorgan and one-time-
Academy-award-nominee Miniature
Driver. Anyone found parading body
hair in public will be automatically
sent to compulsory depilation clinics.
Any refusals will result in deportation
to Germany, Spain or Belgium.
"Get those gorillas outta here," was
the comment passed by southern
California's senior law enforcer.

U

23

NDERWEAR GIANT LAUNCHES_ RADIOACTIVE KNICKERS

Knicker impresario Stan Winters unveiled his most dramatic range of undies yet with the help of Sellafield nuclear plant, writes our luminous correspondent Hoover Sampson. A special elasticated material discovered on planet Uranus is the unlikely secret ingredient mixed into the gussets to form an unprecedented glow said to quash the urges of those who wear them. "We are planning to furnish every professional footballer with a pair of these scanties to aid them in focusing on the game," says soccer's senior head honcho Ivor Bigone. Each pair of knickers costs the tax payer £40 and will retail at £3.99 or two for a fiver.

HOT

DOORS

RUSSIAN ROULETTE

SCOOTER SEX

CUPS

DECOLLETAGE

MINT THIN

ILLEGAL IMMIGRANT

GRANNY PURSE

NITS

NOT

OPENINGS

BAREKNUCKLE BRIDGE

4X4 FOREPLAY

SAUCERS

THIGHS

JUST TOO THIN

RUSSIAN PEASANT

EVENING CLUTCH

CRABS

LOOK OUT FOR! walls

LOOK OUT FOR! suicide scrabble

LOOK OUT FOR! bicycle thieves

LOOK OUT FOR! Knives - they're the new glasses

LOOK OUT FOR! knee backs, they're the new crevice

LOOK OUT FOR! mint thins

LOOK OUT FOR! the homeless

LOOK OUT FOR! the Judi Dench

LOOK OUT FOR! herpes

24

MYFANWY MOORE'S BUGLE BAROMETER

Finally tumbling into the shops:
KAT SPOONER SCHNOFF
(Sweden's answer to Estonia's Carl Stoat)

◆

has designed blinds that mimic the existing scene outside your window. Made of a revolutionary milky soft lurex called Zic, she painstakingly paints the view from your window onto the blind using her own thumb.

No more forgetting where you live!

◆ myview blind £2,400 per sqm from Spac ◆

HEAVY MOHAIR is the fabric to fondle this Spring. B J Yo Ho team it with **BUBBLE WRAP** for a cosy take on last year's apron hat.

Spanish high street chain **BUMMA** *have started a lifestyle homeware line in their virtual shops. All are striking and affordable.*

mucas vases
coffee bean tables
patent leather sofas

yousayvasewesayvase vase
small £6, large £2.

BUMMA

THIS **BEAUTIFUL**
GLAZED BOWL

will be the talk of your table, and you'll be doing your bit for the environment and good causes. Made of re-pressed Latvians the clever people at banishfamish-aid have created something that lactates the ozone and also makes a fantastic altarpiece.

spit bowl 400yen from

YEAHYEAHYEAHRIGHT.COM

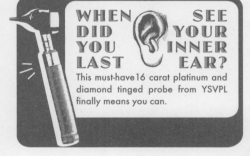

WHEN DID YOU LAST **SEE YOUR INNER EAR?**

This must-have 16 carat platinum and diamond tinged probe from YSVPL finally means you can.

The fall of Ocean's 7 (creators of the sell out 'whore' wedgie jean) have done it again. A fire resistant denim flap extends from the waist up your back, twisting into a sweatshirt hoodie that covers your head. Accessorise with their stash bag in molten brown. Already a waiting list amongst the OC posse. hoodie jean £256 from MUFF

SCABS

ARE THE NEW CORSAGES!
Create your own by falling over.
A day later and hey presto!
Simply peel and fix to lapel/pocket/handbag

We love this striking new idea.

from *La La*

French boutique LaLa have poured scented wax into specially built glass containers. A pretty label completes this boudoir essential.

candle **450€**

ALEXANDER BETWEEN

has again influenced the high/low street. The invisible couture show has spawned dozens of cheap but cheerful copycats of his 'Emperor's Nude' dress. Team it with the new oak and cement wedge from M.I.N.G.E.R.

CLOTHING SAMPLES TOW THE LINE

German scientists have developed a GPS sensitive thread for designers to use in samples lent out for photo shoots.

Editors at top magazines around the globe are protesting this technology, claiming the addition of this thread tampers with the quality of the garment. But fashion houses claim this technology will help them to get samples back from magazines which too often 'misplace' things. "We've lost millions of samples at the hands of editors who think that we are their personal shoppers," said Edward Neon-Brolly in a statement made last week. "With this technology, we will be able to claim back what is actually ours."

New legislation is being considered in the city of New York for laws regarding the handing out of samples. The proposal comes after an incident on Thursday where two women were arrested for brawling over a gift bag at Kevin Clone's show on Friday afternoon.

The bag contained one M.A.C. lipstick in Cyber, (a deep plum hue), a bottle of spray on shimmer, a half bottle of Fiji water, and a "customized" t-shirt. The two women apparently started to physically assault one another when one called the other a "label whore."

All items in the gift bag were determined to have come from last season. This incident is one of over 300 reports of battery reported during the first week of September.

OODY

GOODY

BAG
BAG

28

HE'S JAUNTY.

HE'S GAY

AND HE'S HERE TO STAY!

Rubbish proudly introduces
Jaunty Hun. Our gay gardening
columnist.

GARDENING

A GARDENER'S SEASON: WINTER

Winter provides the perfect time to reconsider and review the garden. Stripped of the shallow frivolity of the spring and summer, the nakedness of the garden's structure pushes forth into full view. This is the time to re-evaluate and examine one's estate.

Trees and large shrubs are the basis to any decent garden, as they transcend both time and fleeting fashionable themes. These are the plants more suited to the park than the plot. Those of us who are unfortunate enough to live on an estate, as opposed to having inherited one, should stick to their tubs and terracotta-effect urns. Urban gardeners turn away now.

Providing the compositional essence of the garden, many of one's larger specimens will by now, have had a good old trim and a nice revealing clip to display their grandeur. This must be a controlled operation. If you're not sure how or when to do it, get a professional in. No Brazilians here, thank you. But while some transient trees and shrubs are there to let one indulge in a bit of fantasy, somewhat like a cheap tart, other specimens should be viewed like one's partner: Untouched and on a pedestal.

A number of our trees at Hardwood Hall including a few rare Elms have been here for centuries and it would be blasphemy to touch them. With their great towering columns and dome-shaped canopies, I get a great deal of satisfaction when my lover gazes in wonderment at their size and girth. They certainly look best left in their natural state and let's face it, any kind of topiary is only really for the brave or the French. But in essence, these trees are the kind of benchmark that every man needs in a garden, against which he can measure both himself and his castle.

Established shrubbery fulfills a similar role; a backdrop with which to frame the garden's summer floral frippery, or to support a little colour through the winter in the form of brightly hued stems or berries. Bright jewels, they sit upon the branches, like enormous chewy pearls and frosty diamonds framing a smiling maiden's face.

In these dark, cold months, the purple berries on the Beauty Berry (Callicarpa) and Prickly Heath (Pernettya) bushes are two of the most flamboyant. Both of these plants almost tremble under the burden of their swollen fruit, although it should be noted that the latter is a bit of a funny chap and only forms berries if there is a male close by.

Forming a rampant thicket if allowed to, these are used to advantage when trying to hide a reedy bare trunk, as without some form of cover, this kind of thing can seem a little dull to the eye. Luckily I am able to have enough land to afford the luxury of not having to worry about "mixed borders", known amongst us country folk as the "Scourge of Suburbia". Nothing worse than a mélange of trees, shrubs and flowering plants. Simply ghastly if you ask me.

Winter isn't solely a time for planning; it is also a time to cherish the garden and to make the most of its barren visual charms. Little can surmount looking out upon frost-drenched terraced lawns on a misty morning, allowing oneself the pleasure of admiring the tranquility and space that only privilege can bring. How lucky am I? And how I pity those poor fellows in the city, with their cancerous air and dirt-ridden allotments. These so-called "urban gardeners" with their sad little plots of land scarcely bigger than our larder. The shame of it. Men, they call themselves, but not by my standards. After all, as my father always said: "Don't trust a city chap with an unplanted acorn in his pocket. He isn't pleased to see you."

29

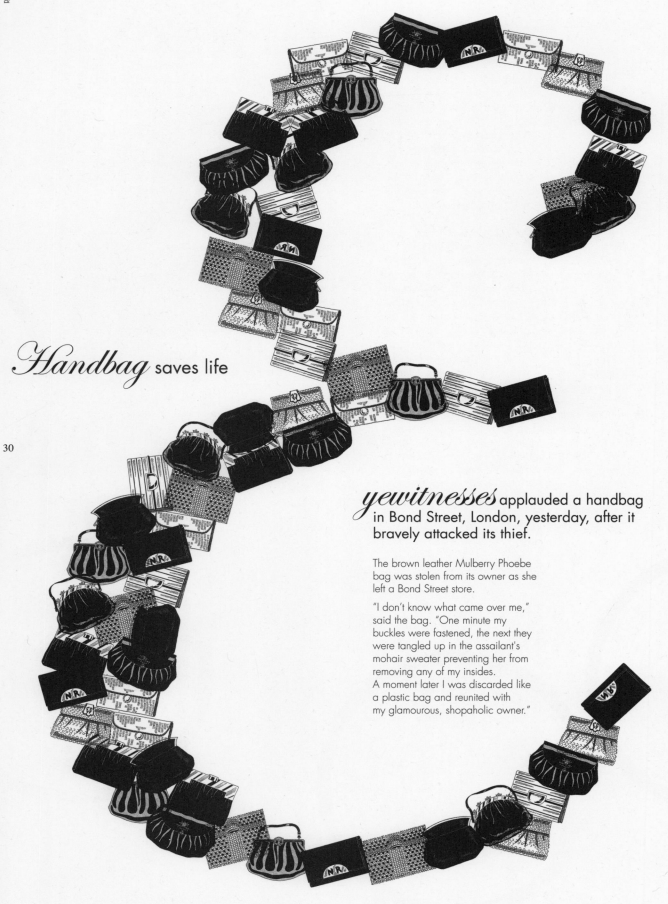

Handbag saves life

30

yewitnesses applauded a handbag in Bond Street, London, yesterday, after it bravely attacked its thief.

The brown leather Mulberry Phoebe bag was stolen from its owner as she left a Bond Street store.

"I don't know what came over me," said the bag. "One minute my buckles were fastened, the next they were tangled up in the assailant's mohair sweater preventing her from removing any of my insides. A moment later I was discarded like a plastic bag and reunited with my glamourous, shopaholic owner."

Illustration by Sarah Doyle

BOTH SIDES

I'm going to dance with fairies in the woods
I'm going to home educate my kids
I'm going to write an organic cookbook
I'm listening to ambient chill
I'm taking special drugs

I'm going to the pub disco
I'm sending my kids to state school
I'm eating a frozen meal
I've got a Take That cassette
I've got some draw

OLD FRIENDS

I'm training in acupuncture it's terribly hard
I can get rid of your cancer with arnica and herbs
I look at your face and can tell what's wrong
Basically you haven't enough inheritance to keep you strong
To think she shopped in Sainsburys for all those years
Not the Grocer on Elgin or Burnstock and Spears
Didn't you know our parents were friends back in the sixties
when state schools were hip and you were dead in your 50s
way before skunk, yoga and Charlie
No wonder she is sick poor child

32

We at Rubbish are proud to present the Bugle's
very own resident poet,

Monsieur Toby Andersen

who hails from fashionable and over priced
West London. Kick off your shoes, pour yourself
a large glass of sherry and pause for poetry.
Chin-chin!

GROWING UP

Middle age is messier than adolescence
It looks better on you young
Your confusion and desperation has only just begun
It all can now be bought and damn I'll buy it if I want
Designer gear, handbags, I'll still look a runt
Don't look in the mirror don't be very nice
Chat about kids schools and property price
We all should have done it in 1998
Made a small fortune down Notting Hill Gate
Fashion is over long live the art scene
With Mojitos Bellinis and all that is right
The eastern European is my wife
It all falls apart so terribly fast
The family we had, the kids that we loved
Second marriage is never the same
The party goes quick
and then you're alone

I WAS THERE

I was at her first fashion show
She used to talk to me
I was there, Yeah?

Her first collection was her ex boyfriend's shirts
Turned into dresses for cute dolly birds

She based her collection on my car boot finds
Ossie Clarke, Biba we were out of our minds

We were such great friends.
Do you remember that night?
We stayed up til dawn and you gave me a love bite

I was there, yeah? I was there.

When you got sponsored it went to your head
That's when you dropped me like a slice of stale bread.
All of a sudden I wasn't your mate
You blanked me for a more important date
But I was there, yeah? I was there.

I was there when it first came out.
When Jesus walked? I was there have no doubt
I danced with Leigh Bowery down at Taboo
We wore Bodymap. Did you?

I dropped my first E back in 87
Danced to the beat at that club called Heaven

I was there, yeah? I was there

God knows they come and go

I was the first to bring it all back
Pick out the winners

I was there before mobile phones
Bros, Curiosity and designer homes

Back then we were all doing it
Once we were kings

Co-written by TA and JD

SO WHAT.

I'm in the film business can't you tell by my wife
She's got a shaved fanny and isn't very bright

I'm in advertising can't you tell by my car
A Porscher a Boxter a big fat cigar

I'm in property can't you tell by my house
It's so oversized you'll feel like a mouse
When the conversation gets big after a couple of drinks
I'll show you my portfolio of castles and things

I'm an artist can't you tell I'm pissed

I'm in fashion so I'm definitely on the list

I'm big in music so it helps that I'm deaf

I'm working class look at my trainers
They're white Reebok.

33

UNEASY LIVING

We live in the perfect

My  are creative

They are my fashion barometer

My style

We've commissioned a for the living room floor

It's by Marni need I say more?

We're a chemical free zone in Notting Hill gate

Get me the we're going to be late

It's only a Tuesday I'm back on the razz

A shop launch, some , it's all so jazz.

The dressing room's cost us an and a

The kitchen's all marble, the dishwasher Smeg

I can't really be d to cook at all

Anyway, I've got a Daily. She's terribly small.

34

We drink lots of it keeps us on edge

Let's pop to the shops for organic

On the way over I'll pop to the dealer

Score me some candy, a faith healer.

My think it's crazy, us staying out late

I'm changing my floor now it's chic for the poor

To have stripped down interiors and an antique

35

I'm a , a shaker, events organiser

I hang out with gods in my Gucci visor

Have you got a ? It's my best friend

In the middle of the I just press send

Did you say Momo's for mojitos at dawn?

Not there again, what a frightful

Co-written by TA and JD

MUSIC

Compiled by Marc Hare,
the BUGLE's Rubbish Music correspondent.

"There were lines on the mirror.
...Lines on her face"

Life in the Fast Lane — The Eagles. 1976 Elektra

Where Rubbish Music and a special guest analyse album covers and their fashion influence. This issue art babe Sam Taylor-Wood chooses The Pretenders 'Pretenders'.

DISC:COVER

RUBBISH MAG So, Sam, where and when did you buy this LP?

SAM TAYLOR WOOD It was 1979 and I bought it from Revolver Records in Crowborough in Sussex.

RM Did you fancy anyone on the cover in particular?

STW Only Chrissie Hynde.

RM Did you have the outfit?

STW I wanted the gloves. There was no way I could afford the jacket as I was only 12-years-old. The look she's working still looks great.

RM Which designers would you say have referenced this cover?

STW Well…those are Stella Jeans and the boots are definitely Marc Jacobs.

RM Who did satin cowboy shirts about two seasons ago?

STW Marc Jacobs again.

RM That is definitely a Hedi tux jacket. I'd say the two guys on the left [James Honeyman-Scott and Martin Chambers] preceded the entire eighties power hairdresser look as popularised by Nicky Clarke and John Frieda.

STW The best hair has to go to Pete Farnham.

RM He's doing Karl Lagerfeld from the front and Suzy Menkes from the back. D'you know what? I think the band's stylist was trying to achieve a sort of punk Wizard of Oz feel. Chrissie is obviously Dorothy, leading Pete the Lion, Martin the scarecrow and James, the tin man.

STW What about Toto?

RM I don't know, but do you think stylist Alistair Mackie has this LP too?

Next issue: Phil Collins' No Jacket Required. For your input and suggestions email music@rubbishmag.com

Word from backstage is...

"Thrash Pilates Keeps backstage babes bootylicious!"

Uber skinny band Test Icicles are to release a Pilates workout DVD just in time for the A/W 2006 collections. Following on from the dancercise success of Madonna in That Leotard, we can reveal the East London electro thrashers have weighed in with the latest easy way to shed pounds. We asked Raaaary Decihells from the band about the DVD:

"We didn't have time to sound check, never mind warm up. We turned up and did our thing. We were really shit and we know that."

Thrash Pilates cuts a normal ninety-minute Pilates workout to a three-minute rollicking stomp, accompanied by any of the band's hits. Perfect for busy/lazy fashion people.

For classes info email Thrashpilates@Rubbishmag.com

Fashion Music!

TIGA- Sexor

If ever there was a formula for being a fashion muso then Tiga surely goes against it. For a start he is from Canada. Is Canadian Fashion Week before or after Australian? Exactly. Secondly, he used to be a Techno DJ. Didn't they torture people in Abu Graib with that stuff? Exactly ditto. Thirdly, is it Tigger or Tiger? It's actually Tiga as in Antigua, Shweetie! Anyway ...take our word for it, tracks from Sexor will be played in approximately 83% of the fashion shows this season, not to mention the after parties, so even if you don't buy this album, you will know every song off by heart come April. Michel Gaubert has a copy so expect a tune or two to pop up on Colette No.8. In the meantime, here is a dinner party quote you can use with confidence: "Who'd have thought Public Enemy, done Chicago jacking style, could sound so fabulous!"

In shops end of Feb. www.tiga.ca

Gig-O-Bites!

We Gig! So you don't have to!

Nov 14th 2005 | The Band - The Far Cries | The Venue - Beach Club, Notting Hill Arts Club

The Venue: concrete floor, a cookie seller, and a fashion stall. This is a loosely organised Swedish leaning club. Nothing Volvo about it whatsoever. Once a month, four live bands, £5 on the door. The Band take the stage. Him, a lot of fringe for a guy with such good cheekbones. Paul Simonon collars electric blue Fender Strat. He better be good to justify that fringe. Her, surprisingly jerky for someone with such a light entertainment smile. Dexterous on the Roland EG-101. Laser cut welly boots, but looking good. Bassplayer could have been Vigo Mortenson with a mullet and I swear it was Keith Moon on drums. A solid back end. The set was more angular than Thierry Mugler's signature. Everything extremely well delivered. Comparisons, hmmmmmm: Sort of like The Breeders with a guy singing and surging guitar and Kills vocals. They belted out a mean version of Eleanor Rigby. Dinner party comment: The Far Cries are a far cry from shit.

Stomping 7" Single "Stepping" on PIA7 records in shops Jan 23rd

www.thefarcries.com

Top 7
7 Inches you'll never find now.

Real fashion insiders don't queue at H&M for Stella; they rock samples from the shows. They also don't do I-pod. preferring the opulence of a fully formed 7-inch for their aural pleasure.
This month's selection has a **Groupie Ho** *theme. Selected by DJ Sven Inches!...A DJ you can trust!*

Rock 'n Roll Queen - The Subways
(2005 Infectious Records)
Stomping chat up record the Von Bondies wish they had made.

Impossible to deal with – Duels
(2005 Nude)
Robotnik jangly ode to going out with a fashion princess.

Waiting for a God – The New Shapes
(2005 Pop Records)
Another pop song about going out with a fashion princess. It seems to be a recurring theme.

If You Want it/ Sexy on the inside - Scream Club/Romanteek
(2005 Whoop-Whoop Rekkids)
Gay electro rap from new gay Whoop-Whoop label.

BB Gun – Bobbie Marie
(2005 Whatever We Want Records)
Electro rockabilly beats with a paranoid rant about having the right look.

Bling Bling Baby - Milk Kan
(2005 Play it Again 7)
Chirpy cockney folk music about bling excess.

Drugs in my Body - Thieves like us
(2004 Hej music)
Ode to a typical east London night out.

TOTALLY UNDOWNLOADABLE!!!!

I RISE AT FIVE OR SIX IN THE EVENING ...

... AS THE SUN SETS TO A FANFARE OF GABBA, A WAKE UP CALL TO THE DEAD FROM MY INDUSTRIALLY TURBO-CHARGED NAKAMICHI ALARM CLOCK AND REACH BLINDLY FOR LAST NIGHT'S JOINT.

I'll begin my waking hours by taking a shower before asking whichever bim/himbo I've managed to cajole back to my stretch loft to leave, as I can't handle the commitment. Then I'll leaf through the plethora of promo vinyl that has popped through my specially modified 12-inch post box. Mostly it's rubbish, sounds like Enya on DMT or some ponce or poncette trying to go 'street' by letting an ADD computer geek in his bedroom put a four-four beat behind their over-synthesised mouse-fart vocals. Now and then though, there is a record or CDR that makes me weep from ear to ear. It's essential that DJs of my calibre respond to promos. I've learned to always be negative in my chart reactions. It keeps everyone on their shelltoes. Next, a breakfast of Olympic champions - one part Berocca, two parts Redbull Ice Plus, with an extra shot of steroids if the shakes persist.

While sipping my cocktail I might call a few other DJs to discuss how cool we all are. I didn't used to mix with other DJs, thinking they were all after my white labels, but have learned to accept their involvement in my life. Sometimes I am too twatted to make it to a gig and it's handy to have wing men so that's at least one good reason to keep them on my ringlist.

Fully lubed, I will ritually approach my SoulDamage's Sneaker Humidor™, an airtight temperature controlled room that I've designed to house my trainer collection. I built it last year with my uncle Vlad and Alan from the pub who did chippy work at the Hacienda. Alan also says he went to the first ever Shoom and carried Runny Dumpling's record box, so I guessed he had the right sensibility for the job. I was right. He performed some of the most exemplary grouting I've ever seen.

The temperature in the SSH is regulated so that my babies stay butt-fresh. My need for Nike, addiction to Adidas and penchant for Puma arose partly from savage peer pressure and in part by a rampantly anal disposition. The anal-ness being very useful in mixing records together. The SSH is a tranquil haven and I strongly recommend that you commission me, Vlad and Alan to make you one. It costs £85,000 but is worth every penny. If my tinnitus gets too bad (I recently shouted at the vicar from the church next door thinking he was keeping me awake with his bell ringing), I will mass produce this sport shoe Shangri La and flog it to every needy sneaker nancy boy in the world.

I've catalogued my collection of 357 pairs into age, girth, width and windmill friction resistance (a windmill being a break dance move which I can't actually perform, but remains one of the sporting endeavours I've planned on mastering in a ninja-like manner sometime soon). There are two or three other categories that I can't remember as I dictate this into my 200 meg Blackberry. One of the problems of a career in DJing is the memory loss. Of the DJ, not the Blackberry. I'm sure rock stars get the same problems as we do. You can only batter your senses with free booze and drugs for so long without suffering the consequences. So I've catalogued my collection of 357 pairs into age, girth width, windmill friction resistance and...hold on, did I just say that? Whatever. Having chosen a pair (sometimes I swear they choose me!), I'll delicately unfurl the protective Goldleaf Sneaker Clingfilm™ (another SoulDamage registered product) and discard it wastefully into the bin. Showing maximum disregard for money and the environment is so cool right now. Giving a flying fuck about any thing is so last season. Or is it the other way around? Whatever. I'll seductively slip the art piece with fat lace on to a box-fresh pro jock sock (from my recent trip to NY - bought 600 pairs) while throwing some shapes in the mirror. I'll start with some light body popping then perhaps do a bit of jazz and tap. This may sound a bit batty but I'll do what I like in the confines of my own trainer

humidor. By now I'm warmed up enough for another pick me up. A couple of lines and I'm ready to spend half an hour regretting my existence perched on the throne.

If it's a Friday, I will soon find myself speeding across Holborn viaduct to get to Stiffies Keep Us Pretty, a new gay club in Soho. One of my protegées, Asbo Diddly will warm up for me. Last Friday I 'psychled' nonchalantly into SKUP and by the time I had reached the DJ booth I was erect and pumping. I remember segueing perfectly from Asbo's last euphoric anthem. The crowd literally gasped and I'm pretty sure it was my mix and not Asbo whipping out his * * * * that caused it. The booth was soon teeming with adoring faces all very pleased to be there.

My driver Horse may have handed out a sandwich bag full of MDMA to the crowd but I'm pretty confident it was my deft blending that was creating such a psychedelic frenzy. My mixing was amazing as usual and having triple dropsied, by five I had the crowd spasming with trepidation as I teased a fresh tech house dish from The Symptoms called 'Bleakdance' into a rough and hard breakbeat cut by The Shelved Corpse Collective (I got a copy before Tongy). Someone said it was massive but I'd say it was even bigger. ONE MORE... ONE MORE echoing around the club is my last recollection of the set. I also vaguely remember waking up in the back of someone's stretch Hummer with two Russian prostitutes arguing about who was going to take me home and rip off my flat. Luckily I had locked the SSH and my record room. I couldn't care less about my other stuff, to be honest.

I woke up with hair on my pillow and I don't think it was mine, and that, in an off-it's-nutshell, was last Friday.

As told to Dan Lywood

FASHION SHOP Obscura

Music doesn't come more obscure than the stuff found in today's front row fashion boutiques. The belief seems to be that if anyone has heard of it, it's well Burberry. Get the Tamiflu, you're killing my look with your populist sonics, you get me? Them beats is chaverage! To prove the point, one of the following records is made up, but can you tell which one it is?

Is it:
a) Gogol Bordella – East Infection
b) Fabio Viscoliosi – Spazio
c) Anything – Off Alex's ipod
d) I Speed Bike – Droopy Butt Begone
e) The French Impressionists – A Selection of Songs
f) Hamas Arc – Muslim Gauze
g) BeeQueen - Gund
h) Aaltopiiri – Panic Song
i) You're in my Seat – Dame Colin McDowell
j) Frankie Sparo – My Red Scare

Answers to music@rubbishmag.com winners receive standing tickets to a show!!!

FASHIONABLE CROSSWORD
FEATURING LOTS OF BLACK, DARLING

CLUES:

ACROSS
1. Translate one part of Pret á Porter
2. Medium often confused with fashion
3. Sunny first name of fashion goddess
4. How the well-heeled refer to their footwear, singular

DOWN
1. Comme's fave rave
2. Dior's hot boy

Desperately SEEKing...
BUGLE MUSIC CLASSIFIEDS:

Underground band seeks well-known fashion designer to make us his muse. We are v. skinny. Have foppish hair with good skin. Influences include Ramones, Stooges and Karl Lagerfeld. PO BOX 6969

Chart topping girl band seeks sense of humour. Despite topping the charts with a Gary Numan track we are difficult to relax in the company of. Especially the chippy one with the lip piercing. TEL 1-800-QUICHE

Jerky post-punk band seeks interesting adjective to be known as. Have experimented with nouns, verbs and adverbs but are looking for something more descriptive.
PO BOX LTRUSS34243

Record breaking Hip-Hop megastar seeks new idea. Steroids have altered my brain and I don't realise I keep releasing the same album. Success has also made me complacent. Influences include Bacardi and shopping and Bacardi. SPEAK TO THE BLACKBERRY 07850 50 50 50

Hiya! Ex-member of hugely successful girl group desperately seeking any kind of career. Will sell bottles of my husband's sweat at Superdrug if it will get me a profile. I am desperate. Help me before my head shrinks so much my Aviators no longer cling to my nose. PO BOX PLEASEBUYMYJEANS

Illustration by James Jarvis

41

WRITTEN & DRAWN BY SIMON ATTFIELD 2005, YO.

You are discovered by a top agency while shopping on Portobello Rd.
+20

You fail to find work and reluctantly take a position at Jessops.
-10

You do a photo shoot for a small fashion magazine AND actually get paid (it's only £50 a page but at least you get to eat - this week).
+8

PHOTOGRAPHER

MODEL

You get your equipment stolen while photographing a grime band in south london.
-10

During the break down of a particular photo shoot you get noticed for your hard work. Nick Knight is very impressed.
+12

You get told you need to lose weight.
-11

Your obsessive looking in a mirror for hours on end affects your work and you miss a string of photo shoots for Prada.
-15

You are selected for the cover of Italian Vogue and shot by Steven Meisel across 20 pages.
+25

You miss your flight and lose jobs at Milan fashion week. pissing off your agency no end.
-15

You date a famous Hollywood heart throb.
+17

You land a Gucci campaign
+27

You release a book of your work.
+13

You develop an eating disorder.
-16

You spend thousands of pounds on a photo shoot that never gets run.
-20

Fall on the runway while wearing a high profile designer. Get world press coverage.
+14

42

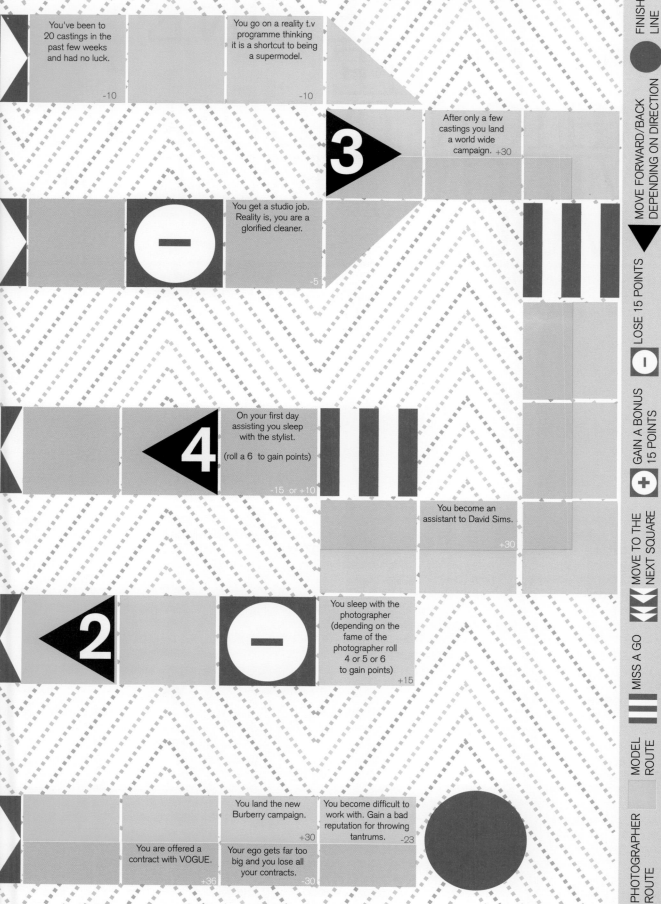

You've been to 20 castings in the past few weeks and had no luck. -10

You go on a reality t.v programme thinking it is a shortcut to being a supermodel. -10

After only a few castings you land a world wide campaign. +30

3

You get a studio job. Reality is, you are a glorified cleaner. -5

4 On your first day assisting you sleep with the stylist. (roll a 6 to gain points) -15 or +10

You become an assistant to David Sims. +30

2 You sleep with the photographer (depending on the fame of the photographer roll 4 or 5 or 6 to gain points) +15

You land the new Burberry campaign. +30

You become difficult to work with. Gain a bad reputation for throwing tantrums. -23

You are offered a contract with VOGUE. +36

Your ego gets far too big and you lose all your contracts. -30

Legend:

PHOTOGRAPHER ROUTE

MODEL ROUTE

MISS A GO

MOVE TO THE NEXT SQUARE

GAIN A BONUS 15 POINTS

LOSE 15 POINTS

MOVE FORWARD/BACK DEPENDING ON DIRECTION

FINISH LINE

Are you the next Kate Moss or David Sims? Choose your career as the model or the photographer and take a walk on the runway to success. Roll the dice and experience the 'highs' and lows of making it in the world of of fashion. The aim is to gain as many points as possible. The winner is the one who has the most success points but beware of the pitfalls which can easily strip you of your jet setting life style.

By Danny Sangra

FASHIONABLE PURSUIT™

43

HEARD THE ONE ABOUT THE FASHION INDUSTRY HAVING A SENSE OF HUMOUR?

SCRATCH THE VENEER OF PLANET FASHION, WHERE PEOPLE ARE SEEMINGLY MORE HELL-BENT ON STRIKING A POSE THAN HAVING A GIGGLE, AND YOU'LL FIND A REBELLIOUS STREAK OF HUMORISTS, WRITES CAT CALLENDER

When jeweller Solange Azagury-Partridge was the creative director of the haute Parisian fine jewellery house Boucheron, she would amuse herself by baptising the jewels with playful monikers such as the 'Milady' pendant. At the time, she told me, it was because she loved the idea that all the suits at the company's Place Vendome HQ, were piercing the hushed tones of the hallowed shop space by muttering ridiculous names. Why? It simply made her giggle.

Azagury-Partridge is not alone in sticking two cheeky fingers up at the fashion establishment. Indeed, she is one of a growing band of designers rebelling against the po-faced, serious nature of style by harnessing a sense of humour and celebrating the funnier side of fashion. "One of the rings in my collection is called 'Ball Crusher'. Some men buy it for their wives," she purrs of a design approach that revolves around a sense of self-amusement. "Of course their wives may not know that's what it's called...but then I find that quite funny."

The private joke nature of Azagury-Partridge's work is something she shares with both Miuccia Prada (who designs things she previously considered ugly to push the boundaries of perceived good taste) and the Danish designer Peter Jensen. "It all started with Mike Leigh," chuckles Jensen whose charmingly discreet designs merely hint at the comic roots that inspired them. "My first three collections were inspired by Leigh's regular leading ladies. The first was called Alison Steadman, the next, Brenda Blethyn and the third, Claire Skinner."

Like Leigh, Jensen is often inspired by tragic heroines. While his S/S 06 collection paid homage to Cissy Spacek's abused ingénue in the film Badlands, style icons for past collections have included the silent screen star Mary Miles Minter (who was murdered in her kitchen) and the shamed ice skater Tonya Harding.

In much the same way that the tragi-comedy film director's observations reveal the apparent mundanity of British life to comic effect, Jensen's collections allude to the curiously banal aspects of the exotic lives of his muses. Take his S/S 2003 comic-strip prints. These illustrated the contortionist-like positions the prepubescent, four-time Olympic gold medallist gymnast Olga Korbut was able to bend herself into. As for next season's aforementioned show, this saw Spacek's trademark freckles deliberately painted on to the bodies of the models sashaying down his catwalk.

"I would love to be able to be completely pretentious about my work," confesses the London-based Swedish designer Ann-Sofie Back. She embraces a subversive brand of humour to critique the industry. Cue her most recent winter dresses. Dripping with appliquéd pearl chokers, glitzy watches and diamond rings, they are a jibe at the hold the accessories market has on fashion. Or her S/S 06 collection - a knowingly chic replay of 80s dressing - sending up the Emperor's New Clothes malaise the industry is occasionally prone to. "I consciously try not to be funny but it's difficult because almost everything about fashion is utterly silly," she says.

Using satire to make a point is something Vivienne Westwood also knows a thing or two about. Last season she may have launched a chi-chi diamond collection, but far be it from Westwood to toe the line. This winter's sardonic offering was clothes printed with a woman lying on her back with the slogan "Fuck Everybody except us" under which, in small print was written, 'US Foreign Policy'.

And then there are those designers who harness the ridiculous and the surreal because, well, they simply adore the ridiculous and the surreal. Take the Dutch double act Viktor & Rolf. Having once released a limited edition scent - all packaging and no perfume - making a joke out of what is largely considered the ultimate fashion trophy, their witty S/S 06 collection literally turned fashion on its head. Not only did the show finish before it had even started (the boys took their bow at the beginning of the show and were followed by a finale parade of clapping models), but the clothes themselves were equally topsy-turvy. Sleeves as trousers, bustier bodices as skirts and up-ended ruffled dresses all reinforced the designers' bonkers message. What's more their dizzifying new store in Milan's Via Sant' Andrea takes this notion a step further by turning the entire boutique the wrong way up. The floor is the ceiling complete with protruding chandeliers and scatter cushions that form banquettes in what would usually be ceiling arches.

Viktor & Rolf are not the only fashion forward types having a laugh. Paris-based accessories label Bless's repertoire of fashion gags includes fur wigs, chair wear (clothes for your furniture) and ear bags. Even the seemingly serious conceptualist Martin Margiela isn't averse to the occasional display of humour. For winter he published a spoof newspaper that sent up magazines such as Heat and Closer with fake paparazzi red carpet shots of divas wearing a 'boa boa' [a stuffed, velvet boa constrictor], and a dress made entirely of handbags.

Still, fashion is probably at its most gigglesome when it collides with reality. "Fashion gaffs are funny because there's a loftiness about it that is really hilarious when it is brought down to earth," says Susannah Frankel, fashion editor of The Independent. She recalls one season when, as the Guardian's fashion editor, she was reporting from the International Collections and dictating her copy over the phone to the copy takers. The result was a review in the newspaper the next morning rife with typos referring to 'Wohji Yamamoto', 'Channel' and 'Donna Karam' [sic]. "When I was working at the Guardian they also ran a photo of Gianni Versace on the runway at his show on the cover of the newspaper. At the time, he was undergoing treatment for cancer of the ear and the caption underneath read 'lovely dresses at Versace, the designer comes out recovering from cancer of the year.' The next day I

received a card and a bunch of flowers from Gianni. He'd written on the note that he particularly loved the front page – which at least shows he had a sense of humour."

Nevertheless fashion and humour are, by and large, uncomfortable bedfellows - particularly in today's megabrand landscape where the multi-millions at stake prohibit most forms of joke cracking. Campaigns such as French Connection's irritating yet nevertheless witty play-with-words FCUK ads and Harvey Nichol's consistently funny approach (its award winning campaigns always involve humour in some way. From the Harvey and Hibby rag dolls of 2000 to this season's rib-cracking dig at the fashion obsessive's preference to forgo loo paper or anything but beans on toast for an entire calender month if it means getting hold of something fabulous from Harvey Nichols) are the exceptions that prove the rule.

While the characters inhabiting the fashion world are in themselves quite funny - notably the former Eurotrash presenter and designer Jean Paul Gaultier; and the former window cleaner turned hair supremo Sam McKnight - most members of the international press corps seem to suffer from a sense of humour bypass. "Fashion folk are constantly trying to convince people that theirs is an industry that is so much more than just pretty frocks and cham-pagne. Everybody's just desperate to inject seriousness into fashion," says Richard Gray, currently Press Manager for Harvey Nichols. He's observed a particularly stern expression the front row editors adopt which he's nicknamed 'the Gucci Grimace'. "Just look at the uniform fashion people adopt: black. How dour. If you wear black you so obviously want to be taken seriously. In fact it's actually quite funny that people want to be taken so seriously."

Of course it's not just the press's bar humbug nature that's preventing the fun infection from spreading further. "Fashion is an international thing whereas humour isn't," points out Tamsin Blanchard, style director of the Saturday Telegraph magazine. "An English sense of humour is different from a German one or an American one so it doesn't always translate. And anyway, fashion folk prefer angst to humour."

While there's no doubt angst has a complex allure to members of the fashion fraternity, casting director Russell Marsh believes the downside to humour is its potential to dilute a designer's vision on the runway. "If you think back to the 80s when Gianni Versace sent Naomi, Claudia, Cindy and Linda walking down the runway, laughing to George Michael's Freedom - what a display of personality that was.

Back then there was much more humour in fashion and the girls had such presence," says Marsh, who these days is exclusively contracted to Prada to cast both its mainline and Miu Miu catwalk shows and ad campaigns. "Of course the big personalities on the runway started to eclipse the clothes. It's why the whole format for the way shows are presented nowadays revolves around an austerity bowing to the notion that models should be mannequins who show no emotion."

What's more, according to Marsh, fashion is an industry uncomfortable with certain displays of emotion, particularly those prompted by a funny encounter.

"There is a real psychology to smiling," he says. "It signifies a connection with the person you are looking at. It's engaging with somebody. But fashion doesn't always want to engage because fashion is fantasy. There's also something about smiling which is now associated with cheesy, chav-style, D-list celebrities."

Suspect classist issues aside, Jensen firmly believes the industry should lighten up. "Suzy Menkes once said she was scared of asking a designer what his or her philosophy of life was in case they answered. She's got a point don't you think?" he says before collapsing into a fit of raucous laughter.

45

WHO ARE YOU CALLING GORGEOUS?

DON'T BE FOOLED BY FLATTERY. IN FASHION CIRCLES IT'S THE ULTIMATE INSULT, SAYS MARY KILLEN

46

For many years my body mass index has been 26.' taking me into the overweight (though not obese) category. Simultaneously my annual financial outgoings have been substantially higher than my incomings. Together the upshot is that I never look "amazing", "to die for", or "stunning". Yet at Fashion Week, which I attended as a journalistic observer, I was surrounded by editors and writers complimenting me in these ways. The same thing happens when I wander into the offices of Vogue looking like a suitable bride for Sir Les Patterson. "Love the look," they say, when they couldn't love it. Rather than inviting further scrutiny, I say 'how kind of you to boost my morale' and swiftly change the subject.

False compliments are not restricted to fashionable corridors. The social machine seems unable to operate without massive lubrications of flattery, huggings and reassurance. During parties one can observe most kisses planted are preceded by shoulder-grippings and body-scanning, then head-noddings of approval. At one recent event the bearded, delightfully portly and pale-faced seventy year old Peter Blake informed me that six people had told him he was looking really well when he knew he wasn't on top form. What is going on?

"Social events these days are dependent on knee-jerk social flattery to lubricate, soothe and ego-stroke," says writer Candida Lycett Green. "No one used to do it, but now it has become a formality like saying 'how are you?'. If you don't tell everyone how incredible they look, you feel like a social pariah. It's ridiculous."

Let's put flattery in its historical perspective. Time was when the English were noted for their reserve and flattery did not occur outside of a couture fitting room. It was considered rude to make personal remarks, even complimentary ones because that implied there was a possibility things might not be good.

"The traditional, English upbringing gave one self-confidence and assurance," says eighty year old Euan Graham, grandson of a Duke and a Viscount who spent his career in that obscure but grand position of clerk in the House of Lords. "In my youth, people never used to feel the need to follow trends or make statements. But after the War the money spread downwards and proliferated. You are then left with an ever-widening class of person who does not know how to think or behave and thinks they should be making a statement all the time, either sartorially or by the expensive gadgets and possessions with which they fill their houses. People want to soak up social reassurance and they compliment you because they want you to say back to them 'Look at you, you are looking well. Gosh, you have lost weight.'"

We are also seeing the seepage into our culture of techniques from Dale Carnegie's 1963 best selling American etiquette book How To Win Friends and Influence People, which emphasises the successful method of reassurance and praise in the workplace. "When I joined the foreign office in the 1960s, it was assumed you always did well; you were never told you had done well. Today one has to tell people they are wonderful all the time," says former diplomat Philip Wetton. "Those who tried the Carnegie formula found how remarkably effective it was and never looked back. The trouble with flattery in the workplace is it becomes unrealistic. Tell someone they are brilliant and they will expect a promotion. It's dangling expectations which cannot be fulfilled."

But when these American encouragement techniques first hit our shores in the early Eighties they were welcome indeed in a world traditionally void of feedback. When the Public Relations boom of the Eighties and early nineties kicked in, it was official: We English were a walkover. Suggestibility was all.
Nicholas Coleridge, Conde Nast supremo, was one of the earliest practitioners of laying on the credit where it's due. In what some might consider a throwback to more civilised, pre email/texting

times, he is forever telling staff how well they are doing with handwritten notes. "I'm not sure if flattery is the right word, but I always try to say when I enjoy an article or a story to whoever was responsible," comments Coleridge on his penchant for putting pen to paper when it comes to a bit of staff encouragement. "It feels natural to me to write a postcard or send an email if I'm really busy. I am reacting as a reader as much as a manager. If I love or admire something, I want to tell the people involved. I suppose I send four or so notes a week; it isn't calculated, sometimes more, sometimes less. I read all the magazines here carefully, so there is plenty to admire. I have never become jaded by magazines, I like them as much now as ever."

But why is flattery and encouragement so particularly vital in the fashion world? "Almost everyone in fashion has job insecurities," says British Vogue's Lucinda Chambers. "You have to ingratiate yourself into the tribe. It is a part of survival. 'You look fab' can be translated as 'Give me a job'." Jessica Brinton, of the Sunday Times Style magazine agrees. "The fashion industry is very scary. Everyone knows they are in the spotlight, being watched by contemporaries checking out your outfit and judging you on it. So flattery is a highly effective way of communicating with people who are feeling insecure. But it is not just furthering your own career, it is also fostering an element of solidarity."

And those who break the unspoken code can cause serious upset. "Normally when someone gets a new pair of Prada shoes it's like a new baby and everyone clusters round them to congratulate and admire them," observes Style's fashion editor Claudia Croft. "This particular person had a new pair which happened to be really flat and frumpy and looked like nurses' shoes yet everyone had to be nice about them and then one colleague, who is famous for his honesty, just said "I think they look dreadful. They make you look like a nurse". You could argue that he did her a favour but what people really want to be told is that they look great."

Everybody wants to be told they look great because flattery has become the currency of the fashion world. "The press are the airy ones," says one of LFW's organisers. "Everything is free for them, the clothes, the taxis, the lunches, the air tickets, the hotels, so they have to schmooze and ego-stroke in order to achieve them. The buyers and designers are more down to earth."

One of the reasons people in the fashion world are more 'sensitive' than others could be due to the fact that fashion is so appearance based. Their awareness of arty things is heightened and they take criticism as an assault on their very being, in the same way praise or reassurance is essential to keeping them on track. Compared to other industries, the fashion world is nebulous. There are no specific targets, no authority figures, no established standards to aim at, and non-stop loose ends to be tied up. You are entirely dependent on feedback from your peers to reassure you that you are on the right track, to say nothing of recognising that you have even done a job at all.

For this reason, an enquiry from a fashionable 'grande fromage' as to where you got your bag can send a pupil at the School of Fashion into a swoon of ecstasy. "Compliments about your outfit from the fashion powers-that-be is a serious accolade and may even lead to a job offer," says one girl who admits to spending entire seasons plotting her different outfits to wear during the collections on the off-chance that she'll catch someone senior's eye. On the other hand, she could have just witnessed yet another empty compliment, as loaded with job offers as a bin bag.

Showing off aside, the object of trying to impress is to make friends so that you can have a happy time laughing and bonding with them. The irony is that looking too great doesn't necessarily achieve anything of the sort. For me, not being perceived as a threat with my defects of fatness and terrible wardrobe can be a huge advantage towards that aim of winning friends, if not necessarily influencing people.

"Yeah," agrees my assistant Matthew Bell as I type these words. "Because the whole thing is, if you look crap, then you are not threatening."

47

Topsy Turvy

**fell
into
a deep, deep, sleep,**

and dreamt of a bush which a
sound did keep,

with ticks and tocks it beckoned her in,

53

and Lily found some

clocks there in,

and when she awoke,

she heard the news.

she heard the news,

the story said, NO TIME TO LOSE.

the story said, NO TIME TO LOSE.
the story said, NO TIME TO LOSE.
the story said, NO TIME TO LOSE.
the story said, NO TIME TO LOSE.

PHOTOGRAPHER: REBECCA MILLER

STYLIST: MARY FELLOWES

MAKE UP: TALIA SHOBROOK

HAIR: LIZ TAW @ NAKED

MODEL: JODIE @ STORM

CASTING & PRODUCTION: ROSIE VOGEL

SHOT 1:
LANVIN'S ROYAL BLUE SATIN SHIRT AND TIE
PAULE KA'S BLACK STRETCH COTTON AND PATENT DRESS
WOLFORD'S BLACK OPAQUE TIGHTS
ROGER VIVIER'S PINK SILK SHOES
FENDI'S BLACK PATENT BELT

SHOT 2/3:
LOUIS VUITTON'S FUCHSIA PATENT COAT DRESS
WOLFORD'S BLACK OPAQUE TIGHTS
PAULE KA'S BLACK AND WHITE WEDGES

SHOT 4:
YOHJI YAMAMOTO'S BLACK JACKET WITH RIBBON LAPELS
AVASHALOM GUR'S ORANGE JERSEY DRESS
FENDI'S PATENT BELT

SHOT 5:
YOHJI YAMAMOTO'S BLACK JACKET
DOLCE & GABBANA'S BUTTON FRONT LEOTARD
TATA NAKA'S RESIN BRACELETS

SHOT 6:
LOUIS VUITTON'S PINK CREPE DRESS WITH JEWEL ENCRUSTED BELT
WOLFORD'S BLACK OPAQUE TIGHTS
BALENCIAGA'S WHITE AND CHROME SHOES

THE END

FASHION- ABLE PEOPLE AND THEIR CLEAN- ERS.

58

59

From left Faride and accessories designer Katie Hillier.
Photography by Chris Brooks. **Sittings Editor** Claire Durbridge.

60

From left Knitting DJ Nova Dando, and fashion PR Mandi Lennard.
Photography by Tara Darby. Sittings Editor Jenny Dyson.

61

From left Dolly and fashion designer Bella Freud.

Photography by Tara Darby. **Sittings Editor** Jenny Dyson.

From left Lorena, actress Thandie Newton and Nico Parker.
Photography by Jenny Dyson. **Sittings Editor** Claire Durbridge.
Thandie wears ballgown by Vivienne Westwood.

64

Photography by Lee Jenkins **Styling by** Su Pollard
Su wearing her favourite all time Giles piece, a dress from AW 2005, and **Giles** with **Nobby** the dog.

65

When high fashion collides with light entertainment, a special kind of magic happens. Designer Giles Deacon and comedienne Su Pollard share their friendship and a few of their favourite fashion moments with Rubbish.

It's a Thursday afternoon and fashion designer Giles Deacon is admiring a pair of 'shoots' while downing a pint at the George and Dragon pub in Shoreditch. The 'shoots' belong to a certain fifty five-year old by the name of Su Pollard. "What do you mean you don't know what a shoot is? They are a hybrid between a shoe and a boot," Su tells an enthralled audience while parading her Santa Fe line dancing shoes with pride. "Do you like them? Richard and Judy gave them to me." She is also resplendent in three watches all worn on the same wrist and one of them featuring a reindeer Christmas motif. The remainder of her outfit is an eccentric mix of black tights, Tammy girl ankle socks, a black rara skirt circa Madonna in Whose that Girl, a white net top, a pearl belt, various brooches and chains, ["can you say they're 'model's own from local locksmiths?' Su laughs as she sips majestically from a gin and tonic], and an emerald green tuxedo jacket with a guitar brooch on the back. "What's that badge there for?" Giles asks Su. "Oh, you'll never guess, but actually I sat on a bit of chewing gum and haven't been able to get it off so it's a natty gum-concealing device."

Giles [who can number Linda Evangelista as official date at society events and pull in super-dupermodels like Linda and Stella Tennant to star in his show AND who, it has been rumoured, was in recent talks with Givenchy] loving Su Pollard's look says more about British humour than it does about British style. Or is that the other way round? Giles's adoration of the highly respected actress and entertainer suggests eccentricity is still at the forefront of what it means to be inspirational. Uniqueness and originality are such hard-to-come-by commodities that when someone so purely 'herself' as Su Pollard enters the horizon, of course she should be elevated to 'muse' status for her new pal Giles [who befriended her, by the way, after noticing they were neighbours]. As he explains, "I have always admired Su's singular style. She is a real national treasure and not many people fall into that bracket."

[ed's note: Here we change interview format and segue into Q&A so as not to dilute the essence of Giles and Su]

Rubbish: Tell us about your first encounter with Giles.

Su: Giles sent me a beautiful 80s/40s boxy, fitted jacket. It was quite a piece. Oh darling, I went for dinner in it to St John the other day, and then I wore it on a hospital visit to see a friend. It was ever so posh. A lot of Giles is haute couture. His studio is a real hive of activity. That dress in the finale for last season, it must weigh a ton."

Giles: It's quite a piece.

Su: The work that goes into it all astonishes me. My friend makes the queen's frocks and he loves Giles's stuff. The most difficult thing is finding people with the skills. When I first started at the Beeb, there was a brilliant costume designer called Mary Husband. She did the Two Ronnies, Val Doonican's suits and all the funny cupboard costumes plus the uniforms in Hi de Hi. I did a show called Take the Plunge — it was absolutely terrible – she designed the costumes every week. I remember a fabulous sequined shorts and matching jacket she made. The only instruction I gave her was that I didn't want to ever look like Bob Monkhouse. Anyway, Mary was my first designer collaboration. I created my own stuff too, along the way.

Giles: Everything of yours has a story, like your jacket.

Su: It's a bit Judy Garland. I love a bit of suede and lace combined.

Giles: You're like the Cher of TV.

Rubbish: What was your earliest fashion moment, Su?

Su: I will never forget being at C&A with my mum Hilda at the age of six and begging for a blue and yellow polka dot skirt. She said no. We've got to break down those fashion barriers.

Giles: The Thames Flood Barrier would be good.

Su: I blame the fashion press. They reign supreme. And I can't bear those tabloid stories where they get five women who are all divorced and make them look hideous. I want to know why every girl, whether she's an artist, actor or performer, feels obliged to wear the same old frock over and over again?

Giles: Bjork didn't. She laid an egg at the Oscars.

Rubbish: What about your fashion philosophy, Su?

Su: If something catches your eye, it's obvious your brain has said something to your purse. A lot of women are timid. I say get rid of your timidity. Explore your imagination. A piece of jewellery that's cheap and cheerful can be fab. Just think it stuff it and don't care what other people think.

Giles: Would you call that kind of attitude 'laissez faire, Su'?

Su: Just trust yourself. Don't take your bloke along if you're off shopping as they'll be bored stiff. Personally I steer clear of blouses and tank tops.

Giles: A loose separate is not for you, is it Su.

Su: Anything with a tie bow is a no go as well.

Giles: You would have hated our winter collection in 2004 year, then!

Su: I like to get a bit of Christmas ribbon — go to Wilkos in the north – and buy strings of beads for Christmas trees. They're cheap as chips, but don't go for the red ones, mind, as my neck got stained. Experimentation is not always good for pigmentation. The most I ever spent on an outfit was £5000

Here on a cabaret dress. It was a plunging hour glass shaped, beautifully lined with hand dyed stones from LA. The only trouble was the beads on the bottom kept flying off whenever I sat on the cabaret stool. Not that I get to wear beady, jingly jangly things much these days when I'm doing so many voiceovers. Being a character in the Little Robots cartoon, doing pantos and white goods commercials. It keeps me ever so busy.

Giles: Guests like yourself,

Giles: What was your mum Hilda's style like?

Su: Slacks with a little scarf and brooch. The older generation would say 'what have you come as?' when they set eyes on me. I can't bear that home counties mentality. At least it's got you being talked about. I've never worn crinoline though, I'd rather drop dead. Tammy Girl at Evans is fabulous. It goes all the way up to size 16 and only costs you six quid for an outfit.

Rubbish: What do you like about Giles's design aesthetic?

Su: What I love most about Giles is his fabulously sideways approach. He's a real professional talent. Let's face it, fashion is a huge billion dollar industry so hats off to Giles for reaching for the sky and doing his own label.

Rubbish: What was it like in your heyday, being in Hi De Hi every week?

Su: You know, when Hi De Hi first came out I was flavour of the month. I went to the Hippodrome all the time.

Giles: He's a nice fellow, Mr String.

Su: Ooh yes, Pete does marvellous things for charity. Anyway, I went on Michael Aspel once in some Terry de Havailland platforms and got so much attention in the papers for it. In one way the comments on my style were fantastic. To go in and express myself like that was quite brave I think.

Rubbish: How would you describe your style, Su?

Su: Eclectic, imaginative and thoughtful.

Giles: It's Skalextric.

Su: I still strive to be never neglectful although I haven't got much hair. It takes me a long time to get something together thank you very much.

Rubbish: Do you have any tips on how to be happy?

Su: You only get into people's psyche if you try and be honest about what you're doing. You can't hide being something when you're 55. Always try to be true to yourself so you can sleep at night. Don't get cynical and above all, don't lose your zest.

Rubbish: What do you think of Giles's personal style?

Su: First things first. I love the fact for a start that he's tall. I love his stretchy jeans and his blazer. But he's also got a brilliant eye for mixing and matching. His glasses are great too. Giles Deacon may not be outwardly flamboyant but obviously his imagination and style is What Women Want. That was a crap film, I know, but Giles is the Mel Gibson of fashion. His shows have been sellouts. He's also feted as a person that is a new force in design and fashion. When I went to his show I couldn't understand why on earth there was plastic down the runway. Well, you never know with fashion, do you? It could have been some kind of style statement. Then a journalist said very politely 'no madame, it does get removed'. I realised then it was to stop it getting all scuffed up. Those poor front row editors obviously thought I was a complete charlatan. Just before it started I looked at that bank of paps and thought 'blimey, those girls are really having

to strut their stuff'. It wasn't my first ever fashion show experience. That was in 1967 for a designer called Margot. All of the models were announced by a chap with a microphone, saying 'and here's Annabel with a handbag and doesn't she look lovely'. But the Giles show was a totally different ballgame. I mean, it was a proper, real live catwalk show. The front row is such a privilege as you can actually see the detail. But they come down the catwalk far too quick for my liking.

makes all the boundaries and

Giles: Guests like yourself, and my bank manager who came on the train to see it, they couldn't believe how quick it was.

Su: And the brightness of the lights.

Giles: In the 80s and early 90s models used to do a smile and a bit of a dance but that kind of thing doesn't really happen anymore.

Su: I suppose you have to think of so many factors, like not keeping everybody waiting or whatever. Who makes all the boundaries and rules, like having to be quick to show your collection? Fashion should have no boundaries. Right, anyone for a cocktail?

And with that, Su picks up her gin and tonic to toast Giles, the charming, cheeky chap adored by all the models who will make damn sure not to miss out on starring in his show. At the Spring/Summer 2006 show in September, had Missy Rayder, Stella Tennant and Shalom Harlow looked a little closer as they reached the end of the runway, they might have noticed a certain Su Pollard and her best friend [the one who makes clothes for the queen] applauding with enthusiasm, gusto and gaiety at every Giles outfit that made its way up and down the catwalk. Cheers to that.

JD

This season I'll mostly be wearing Giles. Catwalk moments from his SS 2006 show.

makes clothes for the queen] applauding with enthusiasm, gusto and gaiety at every Giles outfit that made its way up and down the catwalk.

Cheers to that.

ENDS

RUBBISH FASHION SHOW
AUTUMN/ WINTER 2006

F
F
E

Urgent Memo

Please reserve four front row seats for the incredibles. Not sure who to bump? XJ.

68

Block A

D — 1, MR MOUSELING, MISS LILLY, ALICE, PROFESSOR YAFFLE, MADELEINE THE DOLL, GABRIEL THE TOAD, MR BEN

C — MAISY MOUSE, EDDIE ELEPHANT, CYRIL SQUIREL, TALLULAH DUCK, MOG THE CAT, SCAMPI FINGERBOB, GULLIVER THE SEAGULL

Seating tier @ 178mm high

B — JUDY, DOODLES, MILO, BELLA, FIZZ, MAX, JAKE, MR BADGER, MR RA, MR MOL

A — MR BUGS BUNNY, MR W COYOTE, ANGELINA BALLERINA, FINGERMOUSE, EMILY FIRMIN, BAGPUSS CAT, MR TOAD OF TOAD HALL, BIG EARS, NOODY

lock A - 52 seats + 20 standing

Block F - 52 seats + 20 standing

A — ELOISE, KYLE BROFLOVSKI, KENNY MCCORMICK, RANDY MARSH, ERIC CARTMAN, STAN MARSH, MISS LISA SIMPSON, BART SIMPSON, MRS MARGE SIMPSON, MR HOMER SIMPSON

B — MR MACKEY, JEROME 'CHEF' MCELROY, MR SCHNEEBLY AKA DEWEY FINN, PROFESSOR DEXTER, THE GREAT GONZO, FOZZIE BEAR, MISS PIGGY, MR KERMIT FROG, MR GRAMPA SIMPSON, KRUSTY KLOWN

Seating tier @ 178mm high

C — OLIVIA, BEAKER MUPPET, FLOYD MUPPET, SWEDISH CHEF, PATTY &, SELMA BOUVIER, PRINCIPAL SKINNER, MAYOR QUIMBY

D — COW & CHICKEN, COW & CHICKEN, COURAGE THE COWARDLY DOG, I AM WEASEL, CRAZY HARRY MUPPET, WALDORF MUPPET, SCOOTER FROG

Seating 75mm high

E — R BABOON, DEE DEE, BILLY & MANDY, FARMER OLD MACDONALD, LAURA INGALLS, BABY BOOP, BJ, BARNEY, SAM THE EAGLE

F — PHOOIE, N SAM, G ONE, G TWO, THE HAT, ALD DUCK, EY MOUSE

CO2

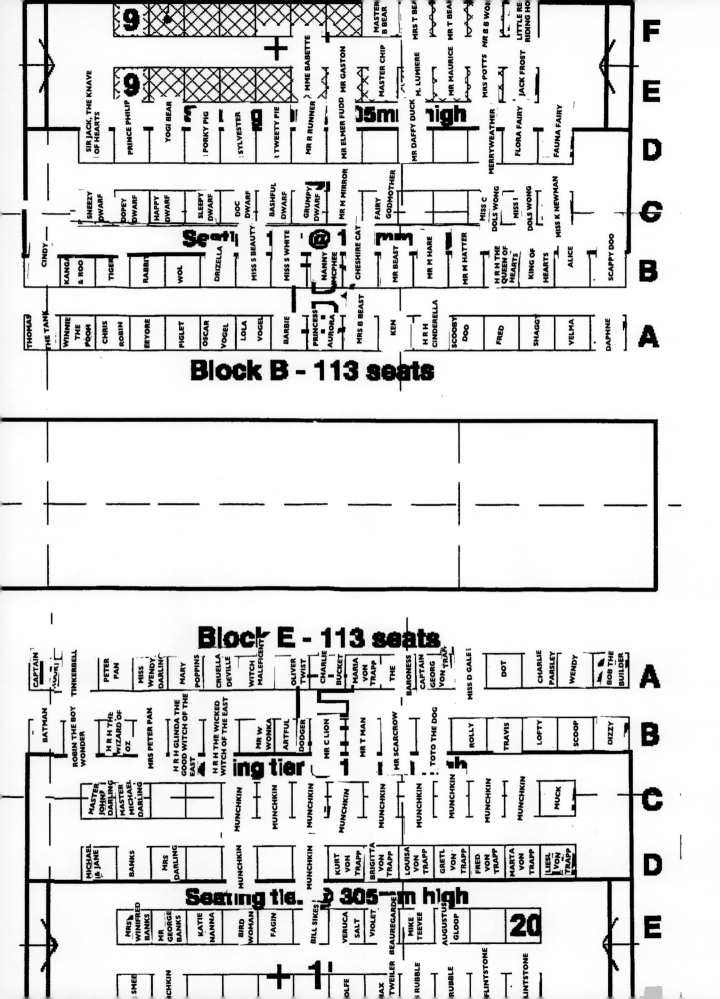

Backstage bins

This season's rubbish

Photography by Rank

70

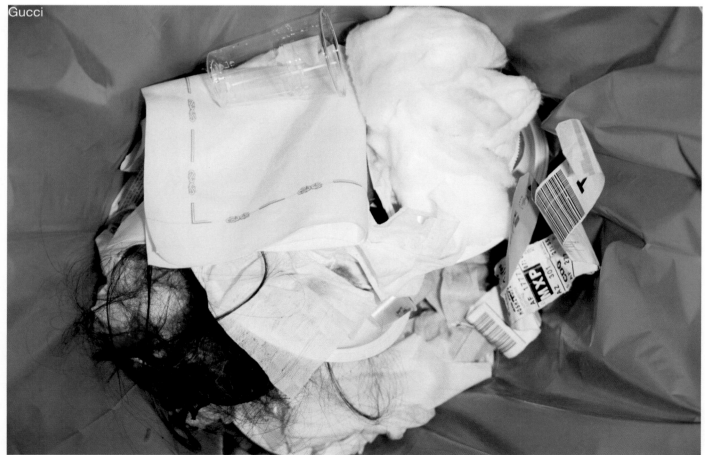

Gucci

Dior

Louis Vuitton

Chanel

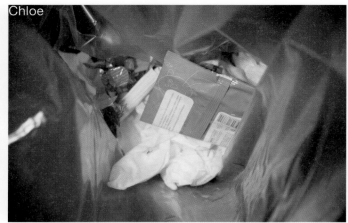

Chloe

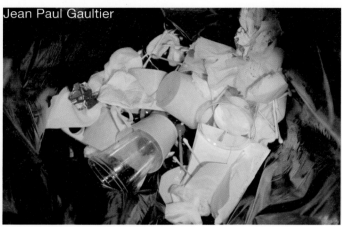

Jean Paul Gaultier

Giles

Roland Mouret

73

Dolce & Gabbana

DOGGY STYLE

PHOTOGRAPHY BY DAN BURN-FORTI
STYLING BY JENNY DYSON

77

"I'm not... Dirty" dog chew tote bag by Antoni & Alison. Modelled by Bucket

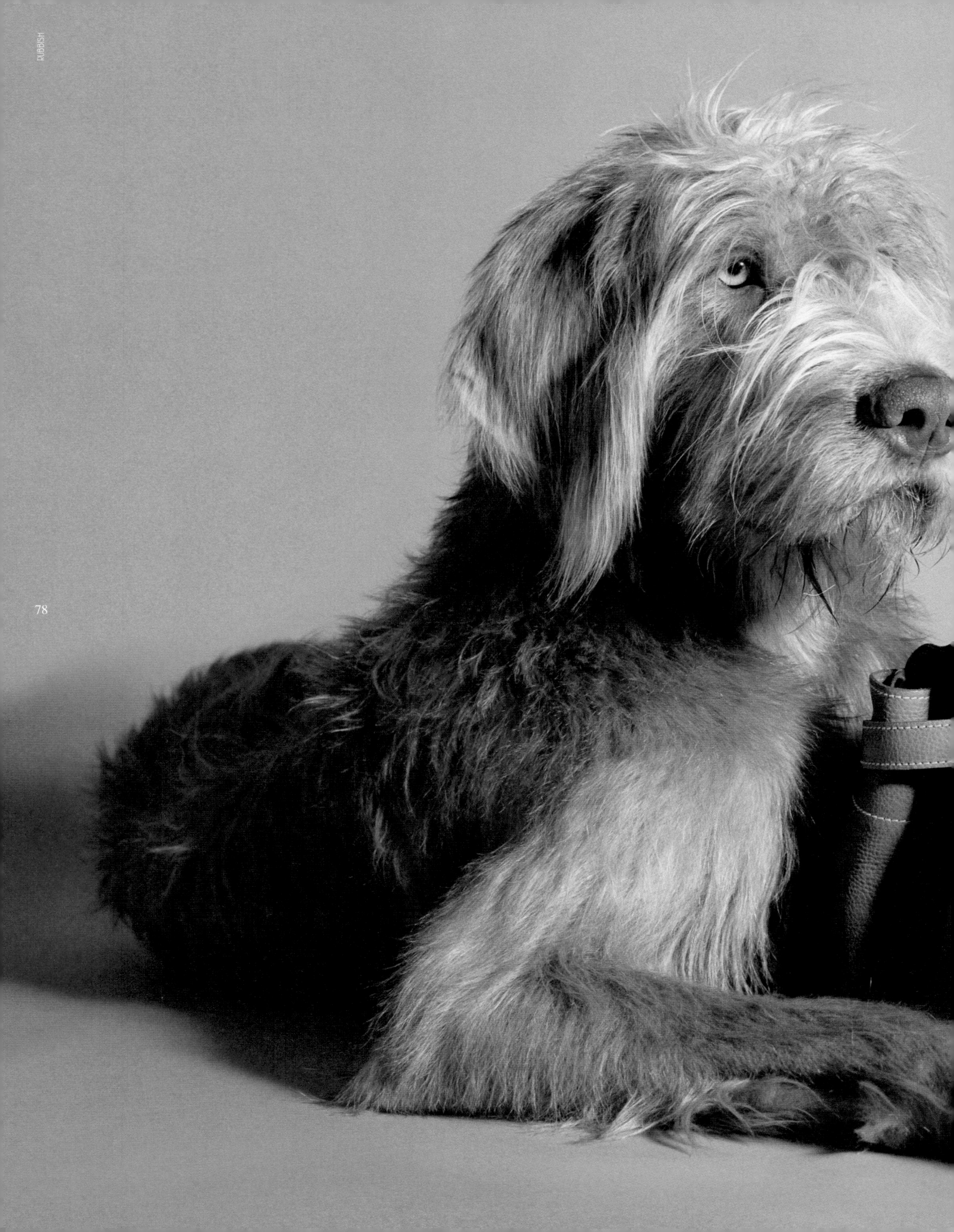

Woof Ledbury bag by Mulberry. Modelled by Billie

Tourist bag by Orla Keily. Modelled by Flute

Bling wing bag by Garrard. Modelled by Buddha

£1

PHOTOGRAPHS BY TARA DARBY STYLED BY ROMILLY MASON

DISHWASHING SPONGE. PACK OF THREE £1.00. ELBOW GREASE NOT INCLUDED.

Crazy Prices!

R.R.P
99p
THIS STICKER IS REMOVABLE

REUSEABLE PLASTIC SHOPPING BAG. GENUINE POUNDSTRETCHER PRINT. £1.00

85

SHOWER CAP. ONE SIZE FITS ALL. COLOUR MAY VARY FROM IMAGE. £1.00

GREATBUYSFORAPOUNDAPOP.HOWROCKINGISTHAT
FORSTOCKISTSHEADFORYOURNEARESTPOUNDSTRETCHER

Autumn/winter's greatest hits
Photography by Tara Darby
Styling by Claire Durbridge
Hair by Robin Pawloski
Makeup by Siobhan Luckie
Modelled by Matilda Kime

87

Oh bother, the ice cream man!
Embroidered dress by Laurie lee
Black coat by Vivienne Westwood
Handbag by Vivienne Westwood

88

STUPID MONKEY!
Grey wool skirt by Burberry
Green tights by Fogal
Brown court shoes by Clements Ribiero
Jumper by Paul and Joe

89

90

Piss! not again!
Blue dress by Preen
Yellow tights by Fogal
Red heels by Adele Clarke

How much longer are you going to keep me on hold for??
Red printed dress, stylists own
Black stilettos by Gucci
Black lace panties by Agent Provocateur

91

Yeah, I should quit.
Black & white blouse by Katarzyna Szczotarska
Blue silk head scarf, stylists own

WHAT TEENS REALLY WANT FROM FASHION....

92

CHALLENGE A BUNCH OF TEENS TO STYLE, SHOOT AND STAR IN THEIR VERY OWN FASHION STORY, AND THIS IS WHAT YOU MIGHT GET

PHOTOGRAPHY BY ITHAKA RODDAM, 16, AND JENNY DYSON, 21 AND A BIT, STYLING BY FLYNN RODDAM, 14 AND ALBA HODSOLL, 15

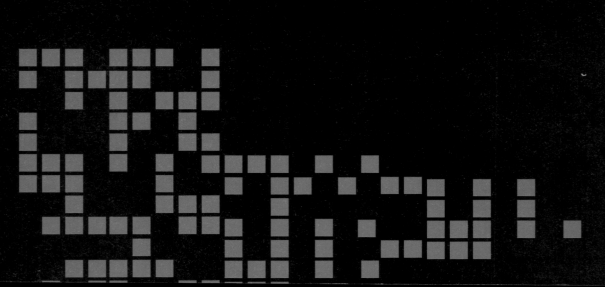

93

Lucy Lyttelton, 16, wears Ithaka's second hand dress from a shop in Bath, shoes and pearls from Top Shop and Lotte's mum's purse belt.

THERE ARE LOTS OF DIFFERENT TEENAGE GROUPS WHO HAVE DIFFERENT LOOKS.

WHAT DO TEENAGERS REALLY WANT WHEN IT COMES TO STYLE?

Well, as I thought this was quite an important subject, I wanted to get it right. So, I gave out questionnaires to my friends and asked them loads of questions. Unfortunately, only one remembered to give it back. (Thanks a lot guys, very helpful).

So I'm sitting here, the day before my deadline, with no material, not much experience and not enough imagination to make it up. So I'm going to tell you what I think.

To start with, what is style? The dictionary says it is 'the distinguishable way in which something is done or worn', but I think it is more than that; I think it is about your attitude and how you consider yourself. It's about being an individual and expressing yourself. There are no limits to how mad you can be, you can wear bright vintage dresses from Portobello or steal your mum's clothes.

But it's also about knowing what not to wear. At 5ft 10in I know that I can't wear certain things, like high heels or kid's clothes, so style is about accepting who you are - tall, short, fat, thin, curvy, sporty, developed or not - and wearing the best clothes for your body.

Gwen Stefani was recently quoted as saying that she was always the fat kid at school who never got on the cheerleading team or got crowned as prom queen, but she said that she always had her own mad clothes and never stopped wearing them.

Today she is my style idol and this just proves to me that it's usually the most stylish people who get a hard time and get teased for being different. But you'll never get anywhere by pretending you're someone you're not just to fit in.

There are lots of different teenage groups who have different looks.

I think when it comes to it, lots of teenagers want to be individual but don't have the confidence. It's always easier to follow fashion because no one can really criticise you for being fashionable, but if you wear something different then there is always the chance your friends might not like it. It is really difficult so most teens stay somewhere in the middle.

Style is dressing to look nice in your view, not dressing for boys or other people. Of course you still want to look nice to other people but you should only wear the things you really like and feel comfortable and confident in.

By Florence Dixon, aged 13

Clockwise from top left: Georgie Hobson, 16, wearing Flynn's blue jumper from Portobello, dress by Juicy Couture, heels by Ына Mia, tights from Top Shop. Bob Gera, 18, wears his own Adidas jacket, James's grey Gap T-shirt, his own Diesel jeans. Lotte Andersen, 16, wears pink espadrilles from Office, her granny's dress, Ithaka's flower chain by Noel. James Richards, 17, wears jumper by Top Man, Nike trackpants, his mate Jake's Pure Cotton shirt and Flynn's sunglasses.

TEENAGERS WANT TO BE INDIVIDUAL

BUT DON'T HAVE THE CONFIDENCE

Left to right: Gabriel Andrews, 16, wears Pringle sweater, Alba's dad's Ralph Lauren polo shirt. Alba Hodsoll, 15, wears "my purple ribbon, pink bangle from Portobello, leopard skin leggings, tutu from Cheeky Monkeys, Ruby's t-shirt from Camden market, Lily's silver high heels from Office. Jake Fellner,16, wears Gabriel's Top Man t-shirt, Gub's black polo shirt and Nike trackpants. Lily Webb, 17, wears fairy wings hand made for her godmother's play, her mum's ball dress by Victor Costa, blue Converse, cardigan by Bonpoint.

98

Matilda Sturridge, 17, wears vintage head to toe. Ruby Reed, 18, wears shoes from Topshop, drainpipes by [...]ress from Whistles, t-shirt "from a gig I went to", belt from Portobello, cardigan from Miss Selfridge, Alba sun glasses.

Jumping for Joy: Lotte, Georgie, Ithaka, Lily, Alba, Ruby, Flynn, Matilda and Lucy

BLiNDFOLD FASHION

Mix up the clothes

1

Blindfolded stylist chooses outfit

2

3

Stylist dresses unsuspecting model

DAISY

What's all the fuss about styling?
Is the stylist's role essential and
crucial to fashion as a whole?
If so, why? In a bid to unearth the
truth, Rubbish fashion director
John Alfredo Harris styles the first
ever fashion shoot blindfolded.
Photographs by Tara Darby

JOE

'I definitely cannot see a bloody thing," says Rubbish fashion director John Harris as model Daisy Lowe blindfolds him with a thick fleece camouflage print scarf. She then sends him spinning around his Hackney studio three times before steering our intrepid fashion explorer towards a stack of clothes and shoes piled up like a jumble sale bargain heap. The heap, by the way, has not been gazed at or interfered with at all by the stylist. Instead, a random passerby called Mizuyo Yamashita has been grabbed for research purposes only and invited to mess up the pile even more. The fashion science project is simple: Contact a gang of fashion PR companies and in-house press offices for a selection of 'casual and smart clothes' so as not to be too specific; Keep clothes in bags until day of shoot, then try and create a rocking look on two unsuspecting models without actually knowing what on earth the 'look' is. "It's not about being blind to fashion," says John as he lingers over the pile of clothes, more than a little nervous at what destiny and fate might send his hand careering towards [he is only allowed to use one hand to find each piece of clothing to ensure no cheating]. Will our fashion director choose something that will look revolting? Will Joe, the male model end up having to squeeze himself into a size eight dress? Will John, whose previous credits include styling many an ad campaign survive the experiment? "People think styling is a short cut to style, but it's not. You can't buy style. The subtle things are the most important. It can be in a button, a print, or a stripe, or the flick of someone's hair." It's official: John is now admitting to nerves. But...

as photographer, hair and makeup crew and models look on, he is confident in his ability to use the fashion force. "You look at styling and think it's easy, that anyone can do it. But it's a lot harder than you think." Having finally selected a handful of garments and four shoes for outfit number one, it's time for a quick breather. For shot number two, hairdresser Robin, who has a penchant for pink, steps in and rejumbles the pile of clothing before John is allowed to rummage. For the final outfit, our two models Joe and Daisy give the pile a stir. Once the pieces are selected, the models are dressed in exactly the items John chose. He even shouts out 'boy' and 'girl' each time he touches an item from the pile to ensure purity and precision are in the choices he makes. And the result? "This is surely proof that the force is with those who see it," says John, jubilant that he's got the je ne sais quoi, the mode magique, La Force. The models aren't so convinced. "I feel like a bag lady," says Daisy as she pulls on an outfit consisting of three dresses and a blouse. "I preferred the girl's sweater to this jacket," says Joe of his white blazer and jeans outfit. Our conclusion? Without the professionalism of our models, the choices wouldn't have necessarily worked as well as they did. "Stylists are powerful because we're all a bunch of shallow style-over-content obsessives," says the very shocked and surprised John. "Basically, if you have the right attitude, you can carry anything off." Ergo, the Rubbish mantra when faced with a fashion crisis?

SHUT YOUR EYES AND FEEL THE FORCE!

103

Joe: "Hang on, this is a womenswear jumper. Hope I don't rip it. Actually I quite like it. Yeah, this one is doing it for me."
Daisy: "Joe's is way cooler then mine. I look like drama school teacher from the 80's. This stylist is well RUBBISH!"

104

Joe: "I'm digging this silver jacket." Daisy: "Yeah, I want it. These three dresses are too much all at once and the one on my head is really itchy."

Joe: "Do you think I look like a snooker player out on the razz?" Daisy: "Milli Vanilli?"

Joe: "Freaky we've both got white jackets. Maybe he's not so RUBBISH after all?" Daisy: "YEAH! This is well tomboy and I'm quite into it!"

105

Hi, I'm the caption writer and if I'm honest i can't remember all these fashion credits 'cause it was all such a jumble on the day. Not very together, is it? I do know that Puma, Thomas Burberry, Dockers, Eley Kishimoto, Karen Walker, Buddahood, Inner City Raiders vs Deth Killers of Bushwick, Miss Sixty, Jaeger, Energie, Tu Mens, Zenga, Paul Smith, Fornarina, Fake London, Etro, CP Company, CK Jeans and Aquascutum were all thrown into the pile, but does it matter where the clothes are from? I mean, it's an experiment, right?

Hair by Robin Pawloski
Makeup by Celine
Special thanks to our lovely models Daisy Lowe at Select and Joe Fogg at Models1

PROFESSIONALLY GOOD LOOKING.

Photography by Thomas Brodin **Styling by** John Alfredo Harris **Model** Steve Bunce at ICM

106

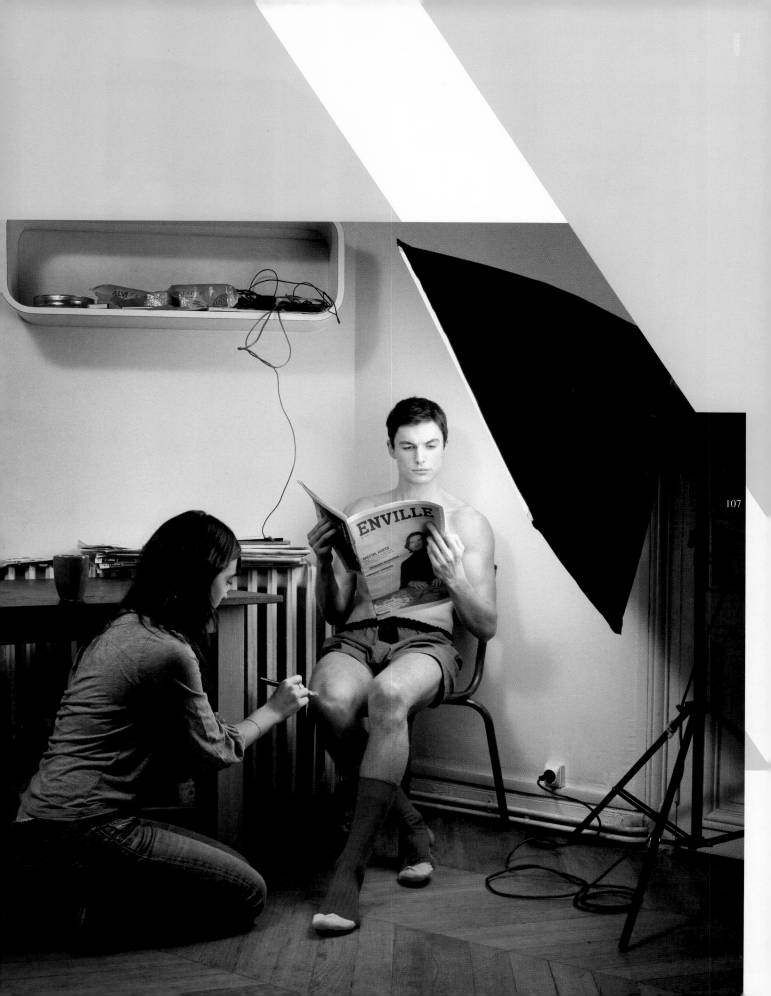

109

110

111

Rubbish Male Order

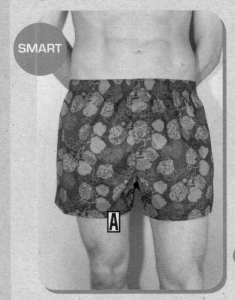

SMART

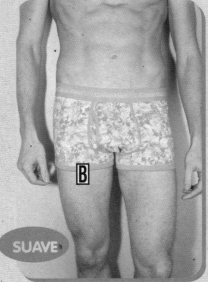

SUAVE

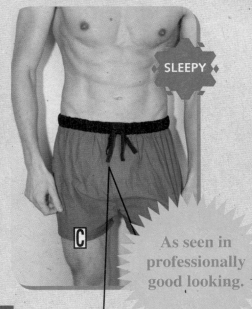

SLEEPY

As seen in professionally good looking.

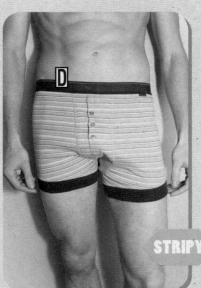

STRIPY

snug

SAUCY

A **Paul Smith -** Boxer short, purple with tree motif.
£22.00 Stockist number 020 7379 7133

B **Calvin Klein -** Floral print trunk
£17.00 Stockist number 020 7290 5900

C **Ede and Ravenscroft -** Burgundy socks.
£9.50 Stock number 020 7405 3906

George - Blue cotton sleep boxer shorts.
£6.00 Available at ASDA.

D **Paul Smith -** Green stripe button fly trunk
£22.00 Stockist number 020 7379 7133

Etro - Pink stripe socks
£27.00 Stockist number 020 7495 5767.

E **Buckler -** Sexy bastard white boxer briefs.
£27. 00 Available at Santos & Mowen,
10 Earlham Street, London WC2H 9LN.
Telephone: 020 7836 4365

F **Eley Kishimoto -** Funky and fast briefs.
Available to order from Eley Kishimoto.

Come On! Call Now!!!

VANITY HAIR

Great Guy Mysterious Hair

ANTONIA WHYATT INVESTIGATES THE MYSTERY OF GRAYDON CARTER'S QUIFF.

113

Graydon Carter is a gentleman whose hair inspires its own set
of follicular adjectives. It wafts. There's a soufflé type quality to it,
a Mozartian puffiness, a dash of Shakespearean foppery. He may be
a successful magazine editor and a man of considerable intellect,
yet it is his hair rather than his opinions that parts people into two camps.
There are those who think it distinguished and others who interpret the
buoyant flickable forelock as a shockingly disingenuous expression of vanity.

The pressing question from both the admirers and the dissenters is:
How does he create the whipped up peak of a hairstyle? Is it a natural
cowlick, or does he apply a bit of mousse? We at Rubbish can only
speculate so we wrangled a few experts to give us their opinions.
"Hmm, could be with a bit of product", says hair colorist to the stars Lester
Baldwin at John Frieda in London. Baldwin is all for a bit of male grooming,
so long as it doesn't take more than a few seconds to apply.

Neil Moodie, fashion hair stylist extraordinaire, took time away from quaffing
the Lilys backstage at London Fashion Week to give us his tips on how
to create The Graydon. "Start with a generous helping of mousse,
then blow-dry it with a small to medium round bristle brush to get all
the edges to flick out. Next take the top portion and dry it back, away from
the face for height. Make a part to one side and blow-dry it over to maintain
the height. Finally, give it a light brush through to fluff it out and don't forget
a misting of hairspray just to hold it all in place."

The mystery as to why (versus how) Mr Carter sports this lofty style was solved
at Claridges. A distinguished journalist happened to be walking down the
hotel stairs when he spied Mr Carter sitting on the sofa in the lobby below.
Shocked and surprised, he observed the crown of Mr. Carter's head boasts
a distinguished Prince Charles style recession, cunningly disguised from the
front by the distracting quiff. Should you ever reach that rare position
of finding yourself above Graydon Carter, it glimmers and shimmers like
the centre of the galaxy, spinning brightly and brilliantly.

NEXT ISSUE: TYCOON HAIR INVESTIGATION

114

Illustration by George Wu.

Hair memoir

by

Diane Pernet

115

HAIRCUT 10p

Lips

Beauty

1 "CHUBBY" BEST BADGER

1979

Fashion legend Diane Pernet's hair is intriguing, unique and very very big. Her pyramid of jet black tresses piled on top of her head is often the only topic of conversation among those in the front row at the collections. Think of a 99 from a gothic Mr Whippy van and you're about there. Here, she reveals her thoughts on her look:

I get the feeling sometimes that there are so few original people in the fashion world, that when people tend to think of an eccentric, it's Isabella Blow. Well here's my Isabella Blow story: A few seasons ago I was waiting outside the Preen show in what appeared to be a monsoon. The rain was getting heavier by the moment and the PR decided to keep us all outside. It was one of those experiences where things get so bad there is nothing to do but laugh. By the time we were all allowed to enter I felt like a drowned rat. No sooner did I arrive at my seat than a, rather loud, blonde Italian journalist came running up to me with her film crew. She asked me if I remembered her and told me how she had followed me around for 3 days with her team. I told her that she was mistaking me for someone else and it became apparent that person was Isabella Blow. Now, honestly I don't look anything like Isabella Blow. For one thing she has flat, shortish hair and always wears lots of colour and a big hat.

I told the journalist if she had followed her around for all those days she should at least have remembered what she looked like. This woman continued to call over her entire crew and for the remainder of London Fashion Week she was always screaming out my name every time she saw me. Last Season the same thing happened again. I walked into a show in London and again this same blond Italian journalist came running up to me telling me how she saw me the other day in a pink dress. I told her that again she had mistaken me for Isabella and that I never wore pink, in fact that I only wore black.

I suppose it is at this point that you want to know just how long I have been so devoted to the colour black. There are many reasons for it. One is that as a child my mother insisted on putting me in bright colours, which I did not appreciate. In my late twenties I married the love of my life and when he was 31 he died in a car crash. It is not that I started wearing only black from that day on: The colour black has always fascinated me. I remember as a child seeing an old film with Anna Magana called "The Rose Tattoo". She was wearing a black slip, I've been addicted to black lingerie ever since. Black is like a tender, seductive hole into infinity.

So about now of course you want to know just how long I've been wearing my hair like this.

116

1989

1987

1979

2005

117

1985

1st. FALL / WINTER EXHIBITION SHOW

1981

Norman Davids 1977

A collection of images courtesy of Diane Pernet

It started a little bit after I became a fashion designer.

Back to Anna Magnani and the just rolled-out-of-bed look: I started wearing part of my hair caught up a bit on one side and just casually falling down on the other. In a little time I wanted to have a bit more height. In fact, truth be told I am only 5'2". I've always been convinced that I was meant to be much taller, Gemini rising I suppose.

Most of my personal treasures were put in Chelsea storage before I moved to Paris fifteen years ago. Things happened and they all got lost in space. I have a few photographs to show you but none before the age of 25. Like most people I used to play around a lot with my look. There was a period when I was totally into glam rock. Sparkles around my eyes, lips and nails and there was a time when I was into black lipstick, pearl powder and black nails. Gradually that lightened up a bit and I even wore Victorian white lace lingerie as outerwear for a brief moment.

It would be impossible for me to go anywhere with flat hair. Each time I go through the electronic device at the airport the alert goes off because of all the hairpins. There have been amusing - mainly in hindsight - stories about that. Like the last time I was off to Gwand in Lucerne, Switzerland. Security guards not only pulled me over to the side but they insisted on calling the police. I told everyone to board the plane. There was a group of journalists from Paris en route to the fashion event. My collaborator and the PR stayed behind to make sure that I was all right. Finally the police woman marched me into one of those charming curtained cubby holes. She asked me what she should do now and I pulled out a long hairpin for her to poke around. What were they looking for anyway? Knives, guns, drugs? She said her sister was a hairdresser and that she liked my hair and that she was very sorry. In the end she disturbed nothing. I boarded the plane, hair intact, and that was the end of it. Happy for that since I was the president of the jury.

It takes about fifteen minutes for me to arrange my hair each morning. Of course that does not account for the time that it takes for me to get into the mood to do it. More than that I am not about to tell you.

Even though I was a designer for 13 years in New York, I have never had any interest in following trends. Recently I was exiting from a John Galliano show and Joyce Ma stopped me outside saying that I was the most fashionable woman in Paris because my hair had apparently inspired Galliano. For my look to become a trend? I couldn't think of anything worse.

Diane Pernet

www.ashadedviewonfashion.com

118

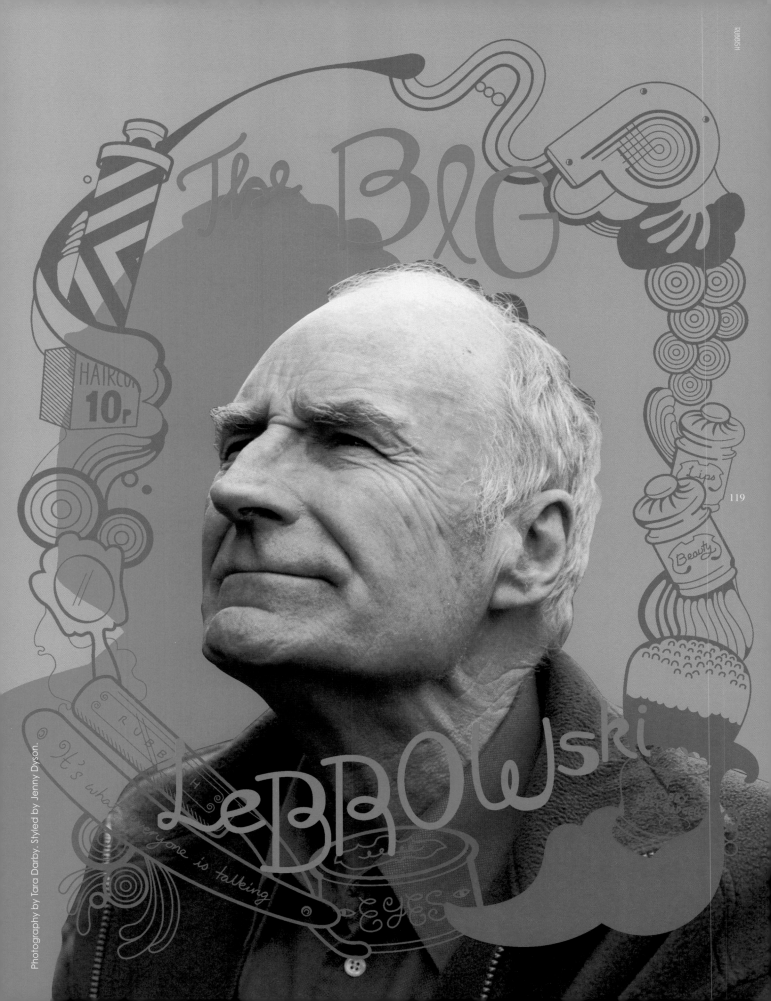

The BIG

HAIRCUT 10г.

Lips

Beauty

119

LEBROWSki

It's what everyone is talking

EYES

Photography by Tara Darby. Styled by Jenny Dyson.

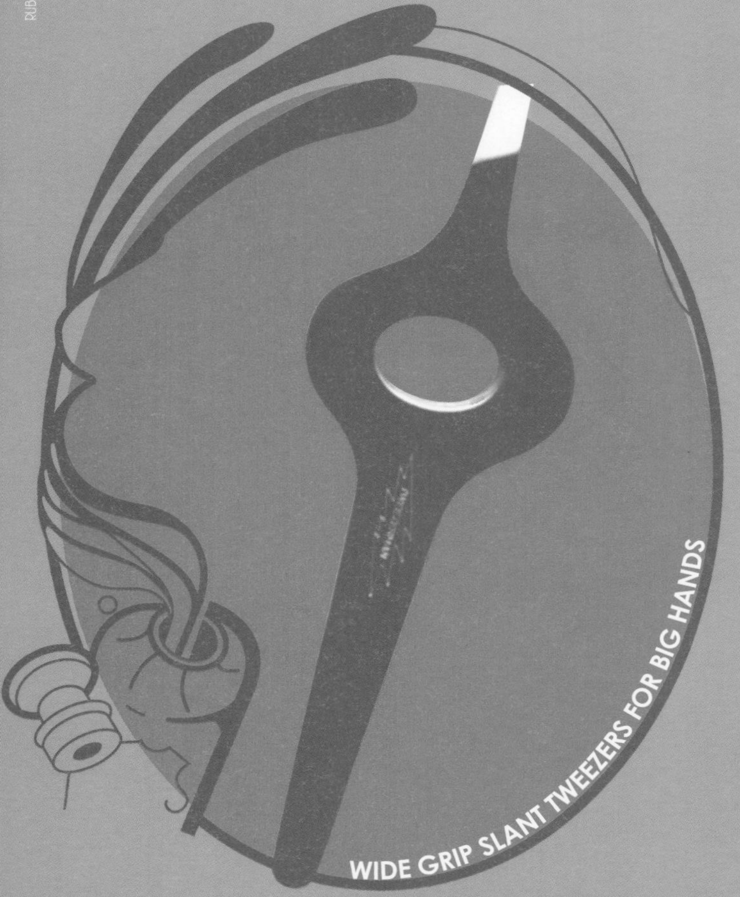

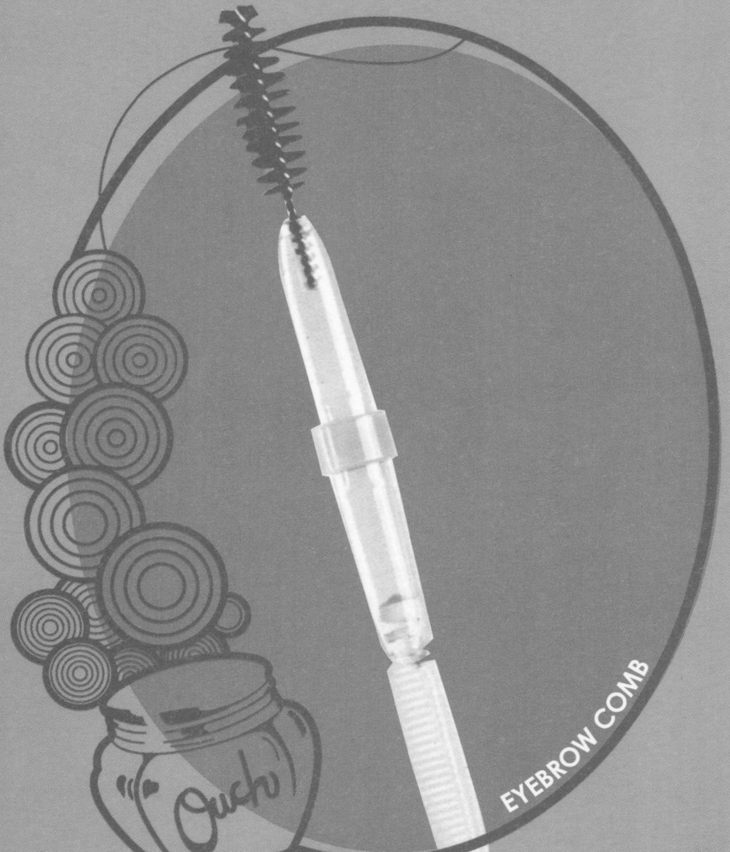

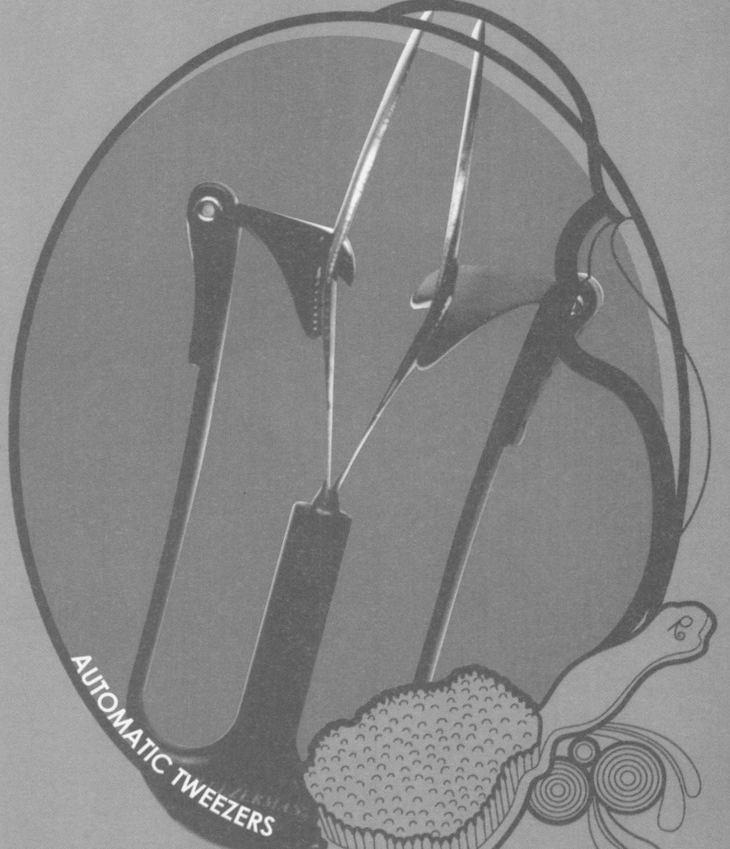

WIDE GRIP SLANT TWEEZERS FOR BIG HANDS

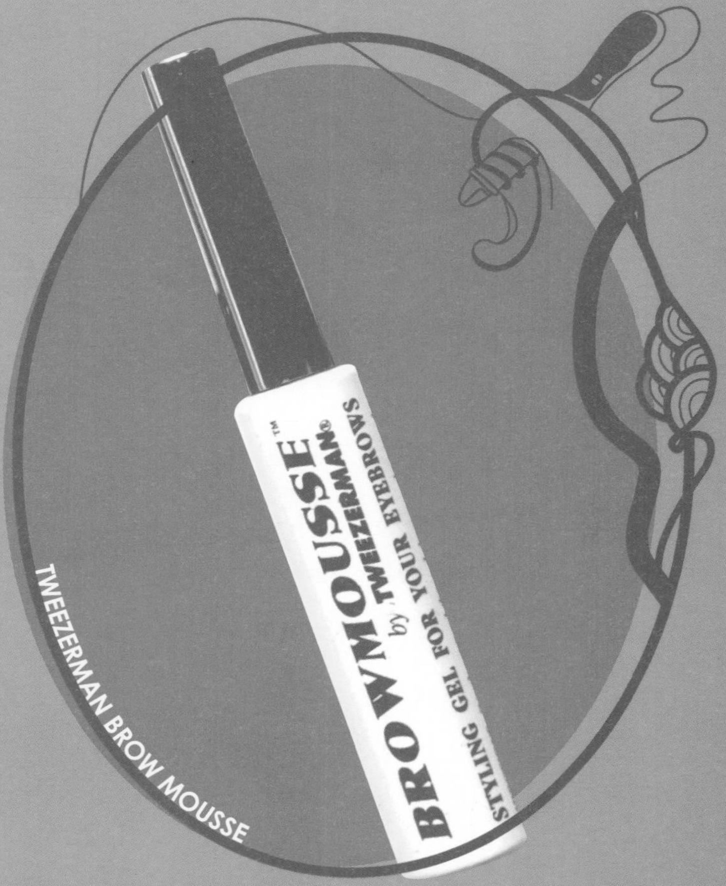

TWEEZERMAN BROW MOUSSE

BROWMOUSSE™ by Tweezerman®
FOR YOUR EYEBROWS
STYLING GEL

120

EYEBROW COMB

AUTOMATIC TWEEZERS

Ouch!

All from a selection by Tweezerman, stockists 02072371007

Why it's good to brow your own

In this over-groomed, lunchtime face-lift era, men are falling foul to tweezers, trimmers and scissors when really it's not necessary. The problem with grooming and primping is it depersonalises one of the most characterful zones on a man's face. If you don't have at least one crazy hair in your eyebrows, you're clearly doing something wrong. As far as eyebrow types go, it's probably fair to assume that the monobrow is not ideal. The look to channel is a sort of graceful, vaguely eccentric yet suitably manly formation not unlike those of veteran broadcaster, Swingometer god and Rubbish brow model Peter Snow.

Loved for his enthusiasm as a broadcaster, and not without his own virile pair of brows, Snow has used his dramatically to underline questions put to politicians during his many years fronting Newsnight. But even his own fine pair has been upstaged by a number of politician eyebrows:

"Denis Healey (Lord Healey, former Labour Chancellor of the Exchequer) has the all-time record breakers: they are breathtaking and very intimidating. They are a warning to any interviewer to tread carefully or they will sweep you aside," says Snow whose own policy on brow grooming is to *"Keep 'em as brow beating as possible: no need for scissors."*

Never tempted to clip his own eyebrows as part of his shaving routine [although occasionally his barber sneaks a quick go at the more wandering branches], Snow is a man of integrity and likes to celebrate his brows wherever possible.

"The more hair the merrier: I have little enough on the top of my head so I make up with it wherever else I can," he says. *"Of course, it is fair to say that all the best people have generous, bushy eyebrows, although I should point out that I like a woman's eyebrows, unlike a man's, to be neatly trimmed and unthreatening."*

Quiet appreciation of good facial hair is not confined to eyebrows, of course. Policemen in India whose moustaches are sufficiently glorious are said to qualify for a bonus in their wages because of the extra authority they wield through the 'tache. Where beards are concerned the list is even more heavy-weight: Darwin, Socrates, Lincoln, Freud, Jesus.

When Eskimos first encountered white men, they called them 'Krabloonik', which means 'big eyebrows'. And why? Because pioneers are real men, and real men have big eyebrows.

Jack Dyson

121

Photography by Zac Frackelton.

Recovery position

Hung over? The fabulous Bistrotheque boys Pablo Flack and David Waddington proudly present nourishing nosh for the Whole Day After the Night Before, complete with glamorous clothing suggestions.

Recipes by Tom Collins **Photography by** George Wu

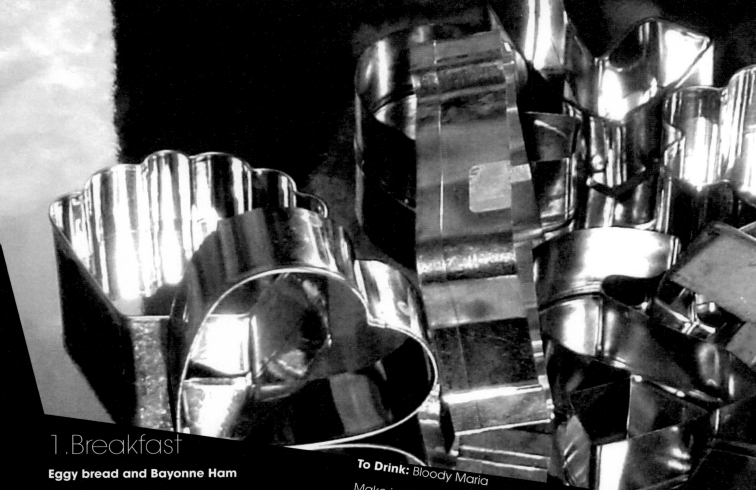

1.Breakfast

Eggy bread and Bayonne Ham

Essentially this is just posh fried bread, which is perfect for soaking up all that acidic booze juice swilling around your tummy. You've also got the slight saltiness of the Bayonne Ham and a good dose of sugar. Therefore the hangover holy grail love triangle is complete: Fat, sugar, and salt.

Ingredients: Good quality Bayonne Ham, 1x loaf good quality butter brioche- sliced, 2x large free range eggs, 40g granulated sugar, Double cream, Milk, Good quality maple syrup (optional).

Method: Mix the eggs, sugar milk and cream together. Dip the sliced brioche into the mix and gently place in a warm, lightly buttered non stick pan. Cook until golden brown then turn and repeat. Meanwhile place some slices of ham under a hot grill and cook until crispy. Place the brioche on a plate with the ham and pour over as much syrup as desired.

To Drink: Bloody Maria

Make just how you would a Bloody Mary (we won't presume to tell you how) but using Silver Tequila instead. Ideally 100% Blue Agave.

To wear: Jogging bottoms and oversized t-shirt.

2.Lunch

Smoked haddock mash.

The ultimate comfort food for a sore head, or even just for those who like their fish and potatoes to be on the same plate.

Makes enough for 2-3.

Ingredients: 500g natural smoked haddock- diced, 1.5kg white potatoes, Double cream, Butter, 1/2 bunch chives- chopped.

Method: Make mash potatoes just like you normally would, using lots of butter and seasoning well. Then bring some cream to the boil and add the fish. When the fish begins to flake add to the mash. Add chives and serve piping hot.

To Drink: Riesling (try some from West Australia's Margaret River).

Optional extra: Valium (only if your doctor recommends it, of course).

To wear: still the jogging bottoms but with a silk scarf tied round your head - mainly to ease the pain but also to jolly up your look.

the day before. Or you've ordered the staff to do it.

Ingredients: 1 pint water, 350g granulated sugar, 1/2 bunch mint- chopped, 3 limes- juiced and zest grated, 70ml white rum

Method: Mix the sugar and water together and bring to the boil. Immediately take off the heat and when the mixture has cooled slightly add the remaining ingredients. Leave to cool for a few hours or overnight then strain and place in a shallow container. Ideally the mixture should be stirred once or twice over a 12 hour period (this will help to give the sorbet a smooth texture).

To Drink: Finish off the Riesling or open another bottle.

To accompany drink: The new issue of RUBBISH.

To wear: Oscar de la Renta vintage silk mumu (boys and girls together).

3.Late Afternoon

A long disco nap

To wear: Ralph Lauren Polo cotton PJ set. Complete with airplane eye mask.

To drink: Courvoisier XO in a warmed brandy balloon to sip in bed before drifting off to the land of nod.

4.Supper

Seared Foie Gras and sautéed wild mushrooms.

Ingredients: 300g fresh foie gras- sliced into 11_2 cm pieces, 300g wild mushrooms, e.g Morel, Pied de Mouton, St George tricholoma, 1 clove garlic- minced, 1/2 bunch chives.

Method: Sauté the mushrooms in a very hot pan with some butter, salt and pepper and the garlic. When cooked, make some room in the centre of the pan, reduce the heat and cook the foie gras for two minutes on each side or until soft to the touch. Add the chives and plate up.

4.Mojito Sorbet

Obviously you are the kind of person who has prepared this kind of stuff

Round about this time you're just about forgetting the hangover and are ready for a night out. Obviously you don't want to do anything too strenuous so may we suggest catching a show at the Bistrotheque's PS2 Cabaret Room. Opium, the demi drag musical comedy by Rhys Morgan, is the perfect light entertainment solution. Don't worry, there's no hectic dancing, just sit down, have cocktails brought to your table, and watch the show. Perfect.

www.bistrotheque.com

email: info@bistrotheque.com

125

DELICIOUS DESIGNERS

Gingerbread men baked by George Wu. Photography by Jenny Dyson

126

127

Butternut Squash styled by Kaye Blegvad.

128

130

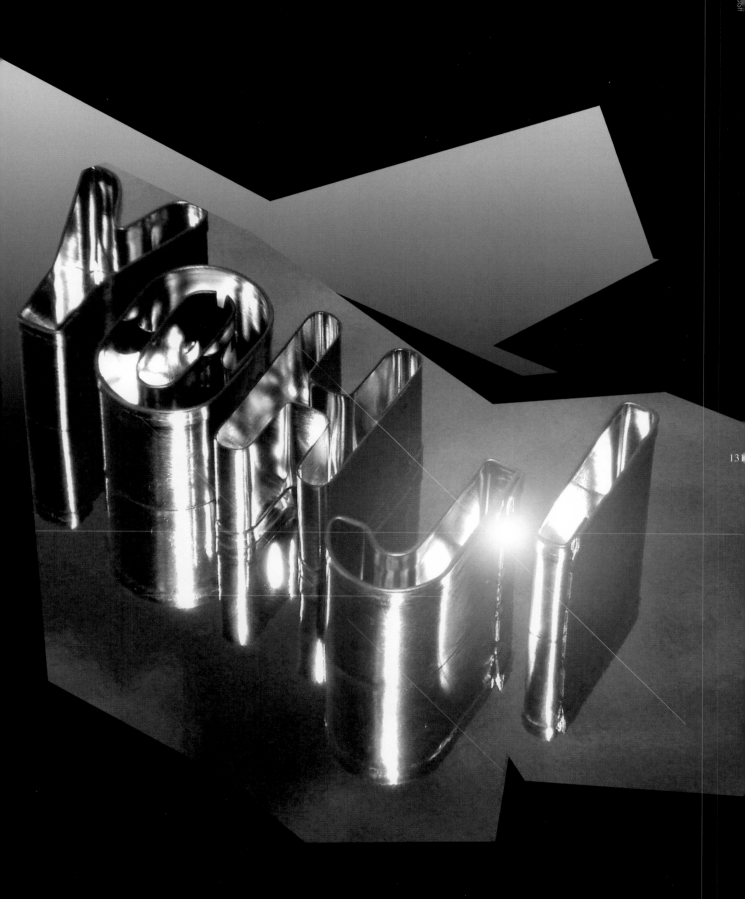

Sweet Potato styled by Kaye Blegvad.

MAKING THE WORLD BEAUTIFUL

Cutting Layouts

★✳ **Introducing Series ❶ of our iconic shapes gallery.™**

 1. **Gisele's breasts**

2. **Frankie's eyebrows**

3. **Kate's hips**

4. **Gemma's eyelids**

5. **Lily's waist**

6. **Claudia's bottom**

How To Use Your Pattern

The metric equivalent is in parenthesis

PATTERN SYMBOLS

—————————————— LENGTHEN OR SHORTEN LINES

 STRAIGHT
Place an even distance from selvage.

 FOLD
Place on fold.

 CUTTING LINE

– – – – – SEAM LINE or STITCHING LINE

 SEAM ALLOWANCE
The area between seam line and cutting line, usually (1.5cm)

 CENTRE LINE

***NEED A LITTLE LIFT?* Look no further than my unique, chic and fabulous body maps ™ . Simply cut out the pattern of your choice from the following pages, take along to your surgeon and get him/her to trace over the template onto your skin prior to anaesthesia. Better still, bring the templates to our headquarters in Tuck street, W1.**
www.youreallylookrubbish.com
Brought to you as a gift of charity from world famous surgeon to the stars Doctor Morph. *"I like to think of myself as an aesthetic philanthropist, enhancing the general public's esteem, almost like a god,"* **says Dr Morph, BCG, OAP, STD, TCP, TSB, TBC, MD, KFC.**

TOTALLY SUPERFICIAL! SELF HARM GUARANTEED!

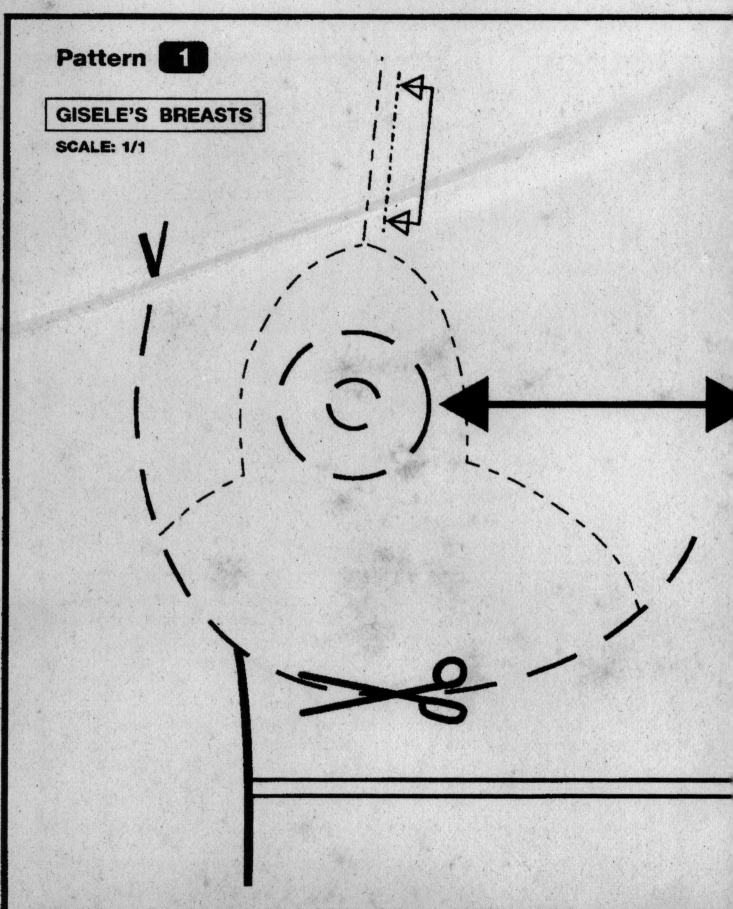

Pattern 1

GISELE'S BREASTS

SCALE: 1/1

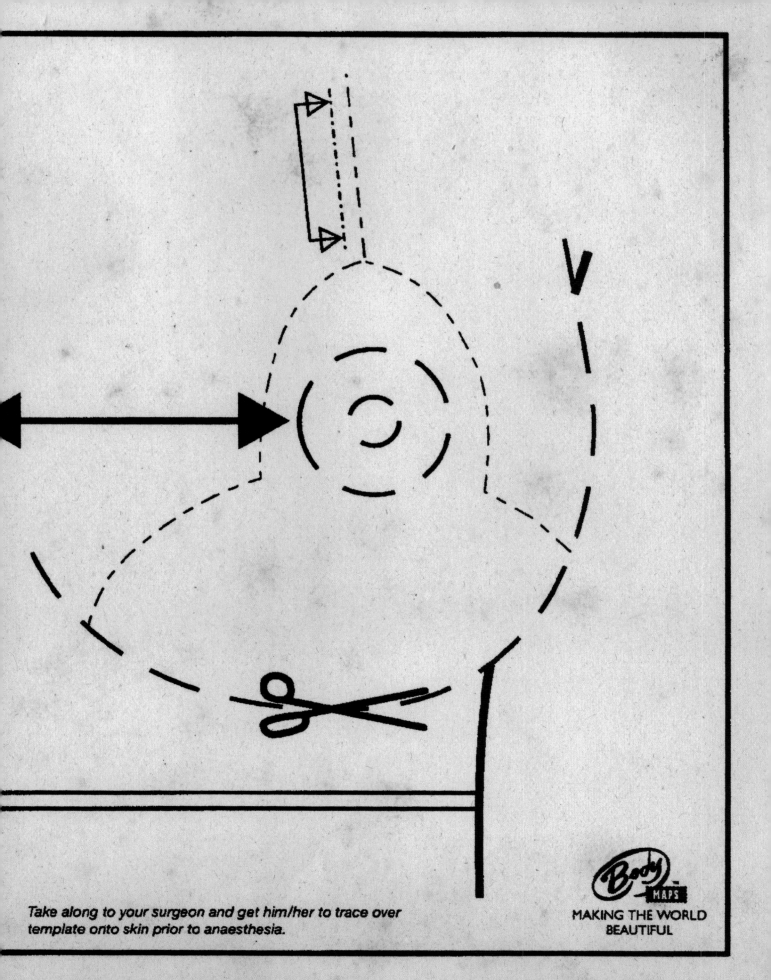

Body MAPS

MAKING THE WORLD
BEAUTIFUL

RUBBISH

Personals

RUBBISH
IT'S WHAT
EVERYBODY'S
TALKING

43 RAINHAM ROAD
KENSAL GREEN
NW10 5
LONDON

London, _____ February _____ 6

136

RUBBISH would like to thank everyone who has been so amazing with their time, generosity and ideas.

Is RUBBISH a book or a magazine? Or perhaps a Bagazine/Magazook? Whatever, without significant input and support from all of the contributors and especially the following people, it most certainly would have ended up in the bin. A big yippee to…

Beth Murray, Bob & Bumble, Briony Hoare, Cat Catalogue, Charlie Parsley Jones, Craig Lynn, Daisy Lowe, Dan and Michelle Burn-Forti, Dorothy Button Jones, Erin O'Connor, Funsho Allu, George Wu, Hannah Weir, Hesther King, ICM models, Jacqui Greaves, Jade Jagger, Jason Bold, Jasmine Guinness, Jemima Loobrush, Jessica Brinton, Julian Broad, Julian Harriman-Dickinson, Kate Finnigan, Kevin Cook-Fielding, Kinna and Greg, Kira Jolliffe, Mandi lennard, Martine Montgomery, Matt Lever, Mischa Richter, Models1, Modus PR, Nick Jones, Nick Steel, Paulina Opoku, Peter Snow, Pierre Darnton, Premier Model Management, Robbie @ Holy Cow, Select, Serena Cook, Simon Bevan, Simon Trewin, Solange Azagury-Partridge, Storm, Take Two, Talib Choudhry, Tara Darby, Terrie Tanaka, Thandie Newton, Worku Lakew, Yorgo, Zac Frackelton

Mwah mwah to retouch wizards Ross and Russ at Goldenshot
www.goldenshotphotos.co.uk

A continental peck to Antoni & Alison, Garrard, Mulberry and Orla Keily for creating the delectable doggy bags

A double cheeked kiss to Miss Selfridge for sponsoring issue one.

And most of all a snogeroo to you for investing your pocket money in total, utter RUBBISH! Xxx

If you liked our illustrations, check out the following websites:
www.purestarproducts.com, www.centralillustration.com, www.kingtait.com, www.mywu.co.uk

2988